A new orkney anthology

First published in 2008 by

The George Mackay Brown Writing Fellowship

In association with Orkney Museums and Heritage, Orkney Islands Council.

Compiled and edited by **Pamela Beasant**

Cover design and page lay-out by **Iain Ashman**

Images by

Rik Hammond

Rebecca Marr (Art and Agriculture - Artist in Residence, 2007)

Chritil Trumpet (Papdale Primary School Artists in Residence, 2006/7)

Lars Abrahamson

ISBN 978-954-8862-91-2

Printed by The Orcadian Ltd, Hell's Half Acre, Hatston, Kirkwall, Orkney, KW15 1DY

A
new
orkney
anthology

THE GEORGE MACKAY BROWN WRITING FELLOWSHIP

contents

introduction

This anthology is a reflection of 2007 – a year's worth of creative writing in Orkney – produced during the first GMB writing fellowship. It captures the breadth of skill and experience amongst writers all over Orkney, and some who visited during the year, from London, Edinburgh and Shetland, to give readings and workshops.

The book is unusual, in that there were no stringent submission rules regarding content, style, or even quality, and the main aim was to be all-inclusive; to show off Orkney writers at all stages of confidence and experience. Some of the work is the first the writer has had published, and others have been caught as they tried their writing skills at workshops and may never attempt anything of the sort again! Others, of course, are very experienced and established, and have submitted work as a tantalising glimpse of what's in the pipeline, or as a response to visiting the islands.

My grateful thanks to all contributors, especially those who, very bravely, have let loose their work for the first time. It is wonderful to have the geographic and imaginative range represented in this book.

Pam Beasant
GMB writing fellow, 2007

part one

UNTITLED Rik Hammond 2007

Andrew Motion

Orcadian

When does the sunlight stop and darkness start?
I don't know what the time is now, or day.
Keep close to me. Believe me when I say
Your beauty drops its anchor through my heart.

Morag MacInnes

Motormouth

He had been expecting the letter since summer. He never told anybody, specially not Bet. She could be a bit crushing. That thing you read, 'his heart swelled with pride' - that happened .

If you ask him I'm oota here, Attie Sabiston said.

You aye say that, said Mrs Heccy Pie.

He can hardly get his heid through the door as it is, if you let him open Shopping Week he'll croon himsel.

He can talk, said Mrs Heccy Pie. She was remembering the Golf Club do and wondering, as she often did, whether anybody kent.

He? Talk? Oh, he can talk, like that man that sells the washing machines, never stops till the money's oot.

The Committee was split. When it came down to it, there was nobody else. Jo Grimond couldn't and the Lord Lieutenant's wife had gone to Aberdeen with a sick horse.

You're just mad at him because o his fancies, Mrs Heccy Pie observed.

I am no, said Attie, I have nothing against his Emporium. If he wants to sell fondant cakes fae sooth full o fake cream that's his affair. I never asked if you enjoyed the Golf Club do? I heard you did.

The Chair, seeing both of her most troublesome members retiring hurt, said that Donald Bell was certainly up to the minute. She got a proposer and a seconder. The motion was carried, mostly because Corinna had to get home to see if her father had set fire to anything and David Puggy Flaws wanted to get to the pub. The democratic process prevailed.

If he had still been in Ongar it would have been easy to nip to the library and pick up a few books. Not here. It was only just dawning on Donald, that island life was lived in the relentless glare of publicity. One twitch towards Teach Yourself Public Speaking and they were offering him tips on projection on the bus. Just like how they all knew about that embarrassing itch, and his new dentures. The enquiries were solicitous, but he thought he detected sly amusement as well.

Don't be silly, Bet said. How's your pruritus means how's your pruritus. It doesn't mean, I hear you've got an itchy bottom, ho ho.

Donald wasn't so sure.

The Emporium had belonged to Jamesina Ratter and her brother. He died, but she lived on and on. For sixty years she'd pulled her hair into knobs over each ear and secured the bumps with kirbies and a hairnet. By the time Donald came to view, all you could see was scalp, tea-coloured strands and cotton wool earplugs. He thought he might get a bargain.

It'll need renovation, he began.

Half way up the window, on a glass shelf, sat three cardboard cylinders of Saxa salt, each of which bore a picture of Saxa salt, each of which…and a round Government Issue tin of dried milk. Above, firmly central, swung a purple twist of fly paper.

To get in, he had to step down into a sort of cupboard, where a cut-out lady with red lips modelled a rain mate, dinkily tied under her cream chin. Then through a green door, covered in adverts for Fry's Five Boys and Lipton's tea.

These'll have to go, said Donald. Never had it so good, eh? On with the new.

She didn't say much, waited till he'd talked himself out. Didna move an inch on the price.

It took weeks to tear out all the display cabinets, every drawer individually mitred, brass handles, and brass framed labels – Two Ply Baby Blue. Ladies' Towels. Kodak 127. Then you could see the shape of the shop; he knocked out the windows, got picture-sized big ones. Ordered a revolving cabinet for costume jewellery. Installed a listening booth. Couldn't resist a lemon formica counter to match the speckledy red and yellow tiles. He would have invited Jamesina to the grand opening, but the Intimation to her Friends arrived just a couple of days before. He put the notice up, of course, but on the door frame. It would have spoilt the look of the windows.

The new sign took up the whole length of Ollie's lorry. Shiny red white and blue Union Jacks curling round the legend: Bell's Excellent Emporium. Just grand.

Attie Sabiston's shop stood opposite. It said Shop on a bit of Basildon Bond in the window. If the paper wasn't there the shop was shut. The window was full of cardboard boxes which said Peek Freans. They kept out the draught.

He'd been friendly to Donald Bell at first because Bell had kept out of bannocks butteries and sponges, as was right and proper. He seemed all right, for a soothmoother. But one day Attie looked across and saw a declaration of war. Six pastel fancies nestled in fluted paper, topped with angelica, cherry halves, candied lemon slices. They were spinning round, slowly, but definitely spinning, on a salver sort of contraption scattered with tiny silver balls, confetti bells and hearts. Underneath he read the fateful words ' We Take Orders for Wedding and Anniversary Cakes'.

Good god, the peedie bugger, said Attie. Given that he had accepted the Lord into his heart, had a total immersion in the sea at Skaill during which he had pledged never to take His name in vain, this was serious swearing. You could call it the equivalent of a brisk salvo of shot over the Emporium's patriotic flags.

The Orcadian published the news next a picture of the Queen and her Maids of Honour outside the Boys' Entrance in a howling gale. Customers came in and said, in the slow way that set Donald's teeth on edge:

Aye...

(eyeing the pudding rice the while)

...I see thu's openan Shoppin Week...

(contemplating the Swan Vestas)

...my my...

(considering Creamola)

...weel cheerio noo!

Somehow Donald felt he was the loser in these exchanges. Still, a voice under his swollen heart sang: they chose you! Night after night he sat scribbling. The final version of the speech lasted an hour. He couldn't bear to cut it.

Donald didn't know his nickname. They're only an insult to the first generation. Once the original Fatty or Sappy or Pishy dies, it's a badge of honour, a Viking thing. Living your life as Harald Half Wit is one thing; being his great great grandson and knowing he was famous the length of the broch line for being stupid is quite another. He was Motormouth. Like all the best monikers, it leant itself to endless expeditions into the heady realms of the metaphorical. Perfect for a slow day at the Pierhead Parliament.

Motormouth pounded down the street, Ongar–speed, and they watched, and said:

Gettan into gear noo.

Crankan up

Indicators oot.

Most of it was gentle funning. Attie was not disposed to be gentle. Stirling Moss, he said, darkly. Graham Hill. Jack Brabham. I'll see the lot o' them oot.

Summer came early, surprising everybody. The bus smelt of hot bakelite. Donald had a machine that made the ice cream twirl into the cornet. Nobody wanted sliders any more. For 1/6d you got a spoon of fruit salad, two sponge fingers, a dot of jam and two perfect balls of vanilla and chocolate, in a flower vase you handed back when you finished. Nobody wanted cakes, nobody sent the bairn to Sabiston's for a cardboard box of sweaty eclairs. The Emporium delivered ice cream. It came triple-wrapped in back copies of the P & J, toothsome tennis balls, multi-coloured.

Attie prayed, apologising for disturbing his Creator with pettiness while there were Russian sputniks and a High Speed Motorway already disturbing His cosmic contemplation. He spent an hour on his knees, gazing at the framed text on his bedroom wall. Vengeance is Mine, it said, in feather stitch with some floral detail.

Then he went and boxed up the stale fancies, took them to the pier and offered them cut price to the Norskies. The heatwave didn't extend to Viking, North Utsire or South Utsire, it was never ice cream weather at sea. He held back the Battenberg. You never knew. The marzipan prolonged the life of the sponge; rain was sure to come soon.

It didn't. Perfect day succeeded perfect day. Miss Wood's class all learned to swim because they could stay in for more than five minutes. The Provost got his golf handicap right down, to the relief of the whole Town Council. The hairdresser's door was wedged open with a curly white wrought iron chair; you could smell setting lotion right the way to Melvin

Place. God told Attie in no uncertain terms that he had to rid his soul of bitterness and turn the other cheek, or He couldn't be responsible for the consequences.

Sunday night before the Opening , the Queen was counting her spots. One of the Pipe Band mislaid his pipes in the bowels of the Hotel. Two Gordonstoun cadets were found in one bunk. Bet Ross opened her door to find her husband's rival on the step, with a bottle in a bag.

I thought you had abjured strong drink, she said.

This is an emergency, said Attie. You could say God bought this bottle, no' me. I'm been acting like a bairn. There plenty room fur a Shop and an Emporium an no bad feeling.

She went to bed and left them to it, first making sure that her man's good shirt and suit were aired for tomorrow's performance, and his shoes polished. She hadn't a clue what time it was when Donald shook her awake. She thought it was part of her dream that he seemed to be talking as if he was underwater.

Then she realised it was serious.

Meet eeth, he was saying. Meet eeth.

Eeth?

Ave lot meet EETH! He grabbed her, shook her. She saw, in the simmer dim, that there were tears in his eyes.

My God, she said, pulled on her goonie and rushed down the stairs.

What's happened to his false teeth? she shouted. How has he lost them?

Attie was sitting in the Orkney chair, contemplating the second empty bottle.

I have no idea, he said, with drunken dignity. I never kent he had teeth. Except commercially speaking.

Donald was behind her. She took his hand.

What happened to them?

I neesd. In t toilet.

Drink always made him sneeze, the great fool.

They ell down e pan. I pullt e shain fore I knew at ad appnd.

You flushed away your teeth? Oh Donald!

Beh! He wailed. My peeth! My oppin eek peeth!

Don't be stupid, you won't be making any speech, you'll be a laughing stock, they'll have to get somebody else. Attie, you can do it.

There was a considering silence from the Orkney chair. Then Attie remembered the Living God.

He stumbled upright

Quick, hid's low tide and late on, no bugger'll be pullan chains noo.

What? said Bet.

If we hurry tae the Sooth End we can look under the sewer ootfall. His plate'll be sittan on the beach, you bet yur life. Tak courage beuy, we'll get you on that platform yet.

A grand Opening. Lifeboat spot on time. Queen radiant after the plastic rollers and hairspray torture. No horseshit anywhere en route, no Guides fainting or cadets puking. Motormouth's speech a miracle of brevity. Everybody marvelled, felt better disposed; he was obviously learning what was fitting. A very nice gesture to thank Attie for his support. No a bad sowl after all.

Over Yesnaby, rainclouds gathered. The wind veered to the east.

Sodden fireworks careered into a milky sea on the last night. Attie gave thanks, under his text. He thanked God for telling him to bury the hatchet. He thanked Him for making it pee down ever since Monday, so his hot pies and sausage rolls were awful welcome. He also thanked Him for Bostik glue, which, though much in demand for model aircraft, can only be considered reliable for fifteen minutes at most, where snapped dental plates are concerned.

Anne Thomson

Newborn

Uncountable
the points of light
that dance in you
*as if the moon
had spilled
upon the ocean*

Unquenchable
the fires
that burn there too
*as if the sun
had plunged
in depths of you*

Unfathomable
the spark
that kindled you
*as if a star
had sealed
its pulse in you*

At Brecht's Grave

On a bench nearby
two old women
blethering
message bags at their feet

sun-dappled, weather-eyed
survivors
of the worst horrors of this century

twa corbies
surrounded by the bones
of philosophers and poets.

On the grave itself
fresh-cut red roses
like a lover's tribute
exquisite
against the plain grey stone.

Such a waste they chorus

I nod in solemn agreement
thinking of the life, the work
that ended.

They wave away such foolishness—

ach nein,
not him, the *flowers.*

Cityscape

so deep and clear
a blue
    this sky at dusk
is a country sky
    the black roofs
of tenements become
gentle slopes of hills
    the darkening streets
fields of stone

a harvest of lights
a bleating of horns

congested and slow, the cars
are docile beasts
in their lanes
lumbering home.

Dancing

My daughter is dancing,
              a slant
of sunlight on the floor
                   her spotlight

She pauses
             to fast-forward taped music
             to her favourite track

I wish I could fast-forward my life
she says,

impatient to know
how it'll all turn out

what will she be?
where will she go?

I dance when the sun's
gone down
when no one can see;

body straining now
to stay on the beat

while in my mind
youthful fingers reach
                 for *rewind*
                     rewind
                     rewind

John Aberdein

The Ferryman

It was a shock, though admittedly logical, when the ferryman asked to look up my arse.

'Your arse,' he said.

That is the kind of brisk remark I was used to from him. *You're talking through a hole in your arse* was a particular favourite of his.

I knew that a *fin de siècle* French vaudeville star made a decent living doing just that, and not just *talking*—

Farting. Farting Schubert. Farting *La Marseillaise* and Rimsky-Korsakov. If I'd been him, if I'd been Le Pétomane, that's the title I would have given my autobiography – *Farting Schubert.* I often wondered how he kept it in tune.

Perhaps he had perfect pitch.

But vaudeville is vaudeville, and this was just a wee Scottish ferry.

He was insistent.

'Your arse,' he said, brooking no denial, if such a phrase has meaning still. I wasn't even on the boat yet. And that was precisely the point. I wasn't on the boat, and I wasn't getting on until he had satisfied himself, so to speak. He had already been through my bags and boxes, my anorak pockets. I reside in a place where *anorak* is not a term of abuse.

'Your arse,' said the ferryman, as the queue got restless.

'Why?' I said.

'Home Office,' said the ferryman.

'Home Office?' I said. 'The Home Office wants to look up my arse?'

'The Home Office wants *me* to look up your arse on its behalf,' said the ferryman, called Mote, or Motte, or something. Probably came over with the Moets of Chandon.

'The Home Office what?' I said.

'Risk assessment,' he said. 'Of all public transport travellers by air, land or sea.

'Risk assessment. Of *all* travellers? I said, stalling for a variety of things, such as waking up on a better planet.

Some in the queue were stamping, shuffling – fingering their belts.

It was a lovely day, I have to admit it. The pathetic fallacy had not kicked in, pathetic really. Instead of louring low cumulus boiling with squabs of rain, like a cauldron of twisting blubber on the deck of the *Pequod*, it was quite sunny and mild, with enough breeze to keep the midges at bay, always a bonus. The hills of Hoy looked close and easily mountable. The last dive-boat was departing the harbour to visit the cold, fertile wrecks. The in-between world was moving modestly through its morning, a cream butterfly down and out amongst fish-boxes, three great skuas taking it in turns to murder an albatross's cousin. The world is full of wonderful padding.

I moved to the back of the queue, to consider my options, if plural.

I got speaking to a woman there, I'd met her once before. She was from Mumbai, very well-educated, a regular tour guide of the Caves of Elephanta. She was over checking the Scottish scene.

'What is going on?' she said. 'Tell me. What is the big hold-up here? My taxi is waiting on the other side.'

She was a Brahmin, so it was a bit difficult. If she had been Untouchable it would have been easy. But how do you explain to a Brahmin lady that a ferryman is poised to look up her arse? Hindus used to be broad-minded, and we all have our tashed *Kama Sutras* somewhere. But now, look at Bollywood. A country of one billion with the collective imagination of a spent euphemism. A cloud slips over the moon. A bush rustles. *Get your kit off* is a cry not heard in the land.

'A bit of a hold-up,' I said. 'Don't know if it's going to clear. Tell me about your caves.'

'The Caves of Elephanta are one hour's boat-ride from Mumbai,' she said.

'Are they very deep?' I asked.

'Don't interrupt,' she said. 'There is no call for interruption. The Caves of Elephanta are one hour's boat-ride from Mumbai. You must catch the boat at the steps below the Arch of Freedom.'

I wanted to query that, the *Arch of Freedom*, but found it safer to hoist an eyebrow, two actually. I have found my eyebrows prefer that, they have little independence.

'It used to be called the Gateway to India, by the silly persons of your nation. Now I call it the Arch of Freedom.'

She was quite a short woman and so did not know that up ahead a ferryman was insisting on inspecting arses.

'When you arrive at Elephanta Island and when you look in, the caves seem very black. Do you know why? It is because they are carved entirely from basalt, a very black rock flowing always from the bowels of the earth. It is a lava, and because it is new, it has very few flaws or cracks.'

'That's good,' I said.

'It is especially good because my ancestors have carved these caves, and created many sculptures on the walls therein, of Shiva as creator, preserver and destroyer, the Trimurti. One Shiva head is fifteen foot high.'

It occurred to me that a fifteen-foot god head would be impressive, but I did not say so.

'The caves are very cool,' she said.

'I think I have read about them,' I said.

'You must go there soon,' she said. 'Fly to India. Let me tell you what the Portuguese did.'

Somebody joined the queue behind me. He was one of those irascible socialists who would make the world immediately better by mending their temper.

'What did the Portuguese do?' I asked.

'Caught all wir fuckin fish,' said the irascible socialist. 'Them, the Spaniards, and the flamin Dutch.'

The Brahmin lady was relentless in her way, and obviously cared little for the species of fish referred to.

'The Portuguese came with their cannon to Elephanta, and wheeled them inside the largest caves. They used our statues for target practice. They blew off Shiva's lower limbs, they defaced a Krishna.'

'Not good,' I said.

'That is why we throw off all imperialism,' she said. 'That is why we have nuclear weapons.'

'The land of Gandhi?' I said.

'Gandhi's *ahimsa* has no role in a modern India. India must have her bomb, to be respected.'

There was a cry from up ahead.

'Dump all thae Pakistanis,' said the irascible socialist, 'then ye'll be safe. Throw in a few Portuguese while ye're at it.'

'It is not appropriate for you to make fun of India's plight,' said the Brahmin. We are surrounded by enemies on all sides.'

Mention of *enemies* made me check up ahead. The cry had come from an elderly artist, our archipelago is moving with them. He was attempting to rebuckle his breeks, while being moved, by the elbow, towards a white unmarked van.

A couple of folk left the queue at this point, shaking their heads, which brought us immediately nearer the front.

'Whit is it all aboot?' said the irascible socialist.

'Home Office orders,' I said, 'arse inspection. I expect it's tied up with Heathrow.'

'A wee ferry tied up wi' Heathrow?'

'Well it's the new bombs, isn't it? Liquid. Spring water, baby purée, everything could be lethal from here on in. Liquid bombs. They don't show up on X-rays, that's for sure.'

'Or body scans, nae doot?'

'So now they're looking in body cavities. In case you've been stashing liquid bombs. Every arse is a primary suspect.'

The Brahmin woman was notably pensive.

'I think it will not be the day for me to cross.'

'Got something nasty on you?' said the socialist.

'I was hoping to visit the cave on Hoy, the Dwarf Stone.'

'The Dwarfie Stane is a very small cave, by anyone's standards,' I said. 'Just enough for two dead people to sleep side by side. But it *is* hollowed out, and it *is* 5,000 years old. Just a one-off really.'

'Perhaps it was fashioned by Hindu wanderers,' she said. 'Our religion is the oldest surviving, 5,000 years also.'

'But no imagery,' I said, 'no carved god head. Just the two stone pillows, plus a block to keep out rats and history.'

'Speaking o' history,' said guess-who, 'an speakin o' rats, I mind I was at a Labour Conference once, it was at the seaside.'

'They often are, I believe,' I said.

'An this guy got up, steely eyes, skull shaved like a billiard ball. Four letter name.'

'Rude? I said.'

'No. Redd,' he said. 'Jon Redd. Unassumin name, but an assumin little creep, let me tell you.'

'You're talking about a Home Secretary we know and love.'

'Aye, right.'

'I hear he speaks very highly of you.'

'The only people Jon Redd speaks highly o' is people higher than himsel. Blair. Bush. But back in '86 it was Neil Kinnock he was slavverin ower.'

'I thought Neil Kinnock was well-equipped to do that himself?'

'He'd been in the job a coupla years, Kinnock, fallin into the sea on camera or intae the bog o his own blether, an the next election was gettin nigh. So up like a monkey in a two-piece suit gets Redd, up on the podium in the Winter Gardens, all gilded an seedy.'

'Redd?' I said.

'No. The Gardens, he said. It was on TV. Shame really. He'd been rantin on podia most o' his semi-adult, had Redd, practisin all the usual tricks: wee joke tae kick aff wi, a coupla jibes at Thatcher, for her privatisations, her foreign garrison costs. Then three groups o' three, a risin rhythm, finishin up wi a clinchin cliché.'

'Nice.'

'But no this day, no in Redd's case.'

'What went wrong? *Falling* rhythm, groups of *two*—?

'Na. The cliché bit back.'

All this time we were shuffling forward. The Brahmin lady was looking through a pair of opera glasses, as the three great skuas dismantled the oily bits on a gannet.

'Tell me.'

'Well Labour had been through dark days, according to Redd, massive factory closures, massive unemployment, massive lack of perks in the House of Commons. We only had ourselves to blame, lack of discipline, lax leadership, longest suicide note in history, et cetera.'

'Always wondered about that one, I said. 'Do they know there's a competition?'

'Who?'

'The suicides.'

'Anyway. So he's windin up, it's the peroration, ye can aye tell, because it starts wi' *but*.'

'*But*—?'

'*But*. But with Neil Kinnock at our helm, we can put these dark days, these storms, these rocky shores behind us—'

'Three.'

'And with Neil as our pilot, we are ready on the runway, ready to take off, ready to lift up—'

'Three.'

'So, comrades—'

'They still used that?'

'So, comrades, climb aboard, raise up your hearts, and cast your gaze forward—'

'Then the clincher, surely?'

'Because, comrades, with Neil driving our train, our express, our wonderful engine of the Labour Party, I tell you now, I can see the shite lining at the end of the tunnel—'

'*Shite lining!* On TV?'

'*Shite lining* live. The BBC are probably holding the tape, against the evil day.'

'Prescient guy Redd, then, eh? Cabinet material?'

'Solid as wood. Spot you a terrorist at three paces.'

The ex-gannet had been ripped to a sticky gristle. The Brahmin lady had tired of the spectacle and was gazing up the hill, where a huge five-storey mansion was being completed, just below the summit, dominating the town. It had twenty-five bedrooms, and seventeen garages, all of them en suite. If you sell your boat and quota for several squillion, and pay off your men with a bucket of whelks, such things are always possible.

'Some call it the Taj,' I said.

'I am sorry?'

'Taj Mahal.'

'It lacks many domes.'

'True. But *like* the Taj, it has one flaw.'

'Tell me.'

'*Unlike* the Taj, the flaw is visible. From all over Scapa. That's why we call it—'

'Scapa Flaw,' said the irascible socialist.

I suppose we were getting into tunnel mode, chummy as evacuees in a London Underground, swapping bits of badinage as the tiles trembled or fell. The Brahmin and the irascible socialist were getting conversant.

Another van drew up and unloaded a hooped shelter, like a pergola covered in plastic. This was in order to speed up throughput, else we would miss the next day's tide. The ferryman was taken off the job, heroic amateur with his thumb in the dyke. In moved the professionals, oozing assurance.

No government can be too swift in attending to fundamentals.

Soon it would be my turn, to expose myself for inspection, for intimate scrutiny, for total evisceration should my betters decree. If needs be, I would carry my suspect innards in a clear plastic bag, and taste them with a teaspoon when required.

Now I am not particularly shy about my arse, *per se*. No doubt it does a better job than my face, in many respects, and is a notch higher on the scale of necessity.

But—

But I decided to swim. Across the tide, across heat-seeking jellyfish, floating voters, across the bull-nosed big wash of Trident.

Just before stepping off the pier, I blew a fart. If I'd had one iota of Le Pétomane's skill, I would have blown a few bars of something rousing, like *500 Miles* by the Proclaimers.

Who knew where I would land up?

Terrorism, and errorism about terrorism, is in our veins.

Christine De Luca

Imprint

Whaarivver we ir, der aye someen nort by.
Only at da pole wid a compass birl, seek
magnetic certainty.

Whaarivver we ir on dis tirlin hemisphere
Polaris tracks wir waavellin. Sho's preened
ta da firmament; a stey.

Whaarivver we ir, nort is a state o mind
wi nae slack: aert's loops taen in,
da tap grafted aff.

Whaarivver we ir, a scanner wid jalouse
wir belangin da wye a stick o rock awns
hits origin.

Whaarivver we ir, slippit lik homin doos,
der a gaet nort. Somethin keeps nyiggin
dat invisible treed.

---

nort by: *towards the north, further north;*
waavelin: *dithering; wavering;* preened: *pinned;*
stey: *firm support, linchpin;* jalouse: *suspect;*
doos: *pigeons;* gaet: *path;* nyiggin: *tugging on*

Da York Boat

The Manitoba Museum, Canada

Dey laid her keel, near therty feet in lent, bielt
her, plank bi plank, a clinkered yoal.
Hit took eicht men to wirk her, rummel
trowe rapids, haul her wi tree trunk rowlers

atween burns. A fraacht o furs ta gadder,
dey snuck up rivers roond da Hudson Bay:
tree ton o beaver, dratsie, muskrat. Dey kent
her wyes; could raise a lugsail or rowe aa day.

Der haerts micht a bön back hame in Orkney
or Shetland, but der blöd raise wi tide an sun.
Bi day, dey laerned new wirds, fan new meids;
bi nicht, fyaarmed fae fiddles familiar tünes.

In Lerrick's museum lins a aald flit boat,
sib tae da York yoals wir nortmen wrought.

---

fraacht: *burden, load;* dratsie: *otter;* meids: *landmarks to
determine position while at sea;* fjaarmed: *flattered;*
lins: *rests;* sib: *related*

Doreen Sinclair

Play with words

Play with words?
PLAY with words?

But words are weighty,
chiming, thud,
tangled, barbed and,
hurled or tossed,
scything shards of comment.

And you tell me to

play with words.

When I read poetry

When I read poetry
I want to reach in
and pluck out
words
which catch my attention,
lay them in rows
match them with a new partner.
Have elephantine
beside gregarious,
My Sweet Lord
by skeleton.

Ella Henderson

Porridge Wars, or Ella's been Bad Again

All the joys of being young on an island croft on a perfect summer's morning were interrupted by the ringing of the 'lady bell' announcing that it was breakfast time. Kind Mary, not many years out of school, who helped put food on the table and made all our lives run smoothly, was standing in front of the black iron stove, ladling grey glutinous porridge into child-sized blue-and-white bowls, hiding the rural idyll pictured on the bottom of each. My mother placed mine in front of me on the table, where I sat between my little sister and my father on a bench running the length of the wall.

'I dinna want porridge... ah'm no' gan tae eayt porridge... ah'm no' gan tae taste yin porridge.'

My mind was made up that not even a suspicion of porridge would cross my lips. My clear blue morning had suddenly taken on a grotty grey appearance as my parents wheedled, coaxed, threatened, even ignored me. My refusals were a challenge to my mother to join battle. It was an act akin to Hitler marching into Sudentenland, and done deliberately to provoke reaction. Since we were on holiday, she did not have to don her neat, navy coat, her perky hat, smart leather gloves and ride off to school on her bike – looking very pretty to my child's eye. A no-school day provided me with an opportunity for a real porridge war. Breakfast became a battlefield. The map on the wall behind the long bench had pins and threads marching across the face of Europe for my father to keep track of that other war.

Eventually, my audience departed. My mother may have gone to regain her composure. Mary, clearing and washing up, went to and fro between the kitchen and scullery. The kitchen was left to my porridge, me and silence, but for the dull 'tock, tock' of the clock on the wall. There was to be no release until I had eaten that porridge and since I was resolved never to eat it, I knew that same plate of porridge and myself were destined to spend the day together. In my soul there was a terrible rage - and a terrible resolve never to give in. How did I imagine that such behaviour was going to earn me the love I felt I had lost when my little sister was born? Such warped, small-child thinking was what had brought about the ruination of my perfect sunshiny day. I had chosen this course of action.

My resolve not to eat the porridge never wavered, and alone in the tock-tocking silence of the kitchen, I contemplated tipping it into that revolting slop-bucket under the sink in the scullery with the crusts of bread, leftover tea leaves and vegetable peelings suitable for mixing in with the mash for the hens. One small bowl of porridge would never be noticed. This plan of action did seem to offer the possibility of escape. However, my mother reappeared and removed me and my porridge to the dairy, because my presence in the kitchen was impeding progress through the daily chores. She carried my bowl.

'Eat your porridge and you can go and play' was the burden of her message. Could she not understand that I meant 'never' when I said it? Could she not understand that each threat only strengthened my resolve not to allow even the merest morsel to cross my lips? With a determination equalling my own she walked out, leaving my stony heart and me.

For how long did I sit at that table, in that small room with, to my right, the separator, whose handle I had been happy to help turn in order to get the milk ready for the calves. As well as the separator, there were fat-bellied brown jars filling with cream for making butter and also, behind me, in a large maroon-coloured 'press' with deep shelves, sat vast enamel basins full of milk on which the cream would rise to be skimmed off in thick layers to go into the brown gathering-jars. Also on these shelves were big basins filled with quantities of rhubarb cut into endless one-inch pieces, soaking up precious wartime sugar rations. The basins were often raided by us children who were scolded for doing it, for all this fruit and sugar was destined to be turned into jam.

Whilst my porridge and I occupied that small dairy my thoughts may have wandered over the contents of the room, which was acting as my prison, but in my heart was rage and resentment, and in my mind a grim determination for my will to triumph over my mother's.... unless.... but there was no possibility of any unless. If only I could be gathered into her warm embrace and shed tears of relief and know, beyond doubt, that I was loved and forgiven, then I could, and would, eat that porridge. I truly would if only I knew she really loved me. I needed her to prove that. In my mind I knew this to be an impossible dream, though I did not associate that impossibility with my conduct. Indeed, iron entered my soul and my resolve was strengthened.

When my mother returned it was to announce my removal to the ben-end. Perhaps the dairy was needed for purposes of kirning, but more likely it was time to dismantle, wash and pour scalding water over the separator to make it clean and ready for the next milking – a twice-daily procedure. Ben was the largest room in the house and served as both sitting room and bedroom. It had three windows: one looking east over the sea, one looking west with an immediate view of my mother's pretty, well-tended little garden, and one small low southern-facing window, with an unimportant bit of grass immediately below it. They were all sash-windows. The small southern-facing one was so conveniently low that even a child could open it. Yes…. a child could open it.

I did not spend long surveying my new, larger prison. My guilt must be confessed. I did engineer my escape by pouring my porridge out of that window. I climbed on the window-sill and tipped it, with its accompanying milk, onto the grass below. What a shameful, unforgivable action. Could I really boldly appear with a clean bowl and tell a lie? Could I really do something as enormously bad as that? I did. I really, actually did. Standing there in the scullery off the kitchen, with Mary standing at the sink, I held up to my mother my empty bowl, with that very English scene in blue and white now clearly visible again, and said, 'Ah've feeneeshed me porridge'. The door behind my mother was flung open and the voices of my big brother and little sister said, 'Ella's thrown her porridge oot o' the window'.

Never in all my contemplations of possible outcomes had I considered such a betrayal. A prolonged and enormous silence filled that scullery, which was, at that moment, the whole world. The silence was ominous.

'Follow me,' said my mother in a voice that felt to me like cold steel. The long corridor which ran the length of the house had somehow grown twice as long.

There, in the ben-end, the room associated with peace and fun and yes, even affection, my mother sat in the deep-red plush armchair, the very same armchair in which she had held all three of us in a warm embrace and rescued Santa and Christmas and made them real for me forever – for she was a gifted storyteller – and now… and now I knelt before her with the palms of my hands together, and my fingers pointing heavenwards.

'Repeat after me: *forgive me, Lord, for refusing to eat my porridge.*'

'Please God, forgive me….' I repeated, whilst thinking, 'I hate porridge, I hate God,' and a still, quiet thought came, 'and I think I hate Mummy.'

I had no feeling of contrition. I dismissed all feelings of guilt about cheating and lying with each phrase which was repeated.

'*Please God forgive me for cheating.*'

'Please God forgive me for cheating,' came my small voice.

My thoughts grew more insistent. They grew to a shout in my head.

'Please God forgive me…. for lying.'

Hate… hate… hate went the voice in my head.

'And please God make me a good girl, for Jesus' sake. Amen.'

By this time I really did hate not just porridge or God. I definitely hated my mother too. And what of my brother and sister?

Oh what a change had come over my day. I was an outcast. Even if my brother and sister had tried to befriend me, I wanted to be on my own. Disconsolately, I wandered through the bright day. The sky eventually reminded me that it was still blue; daisies bloomed and could still be made into daisy-chains; the buttercups and dandelions were just as gloriously yellow as ever, and the white 'milk' from the dandelion stalks still made black stains on my hands. The real world was just as real as it was before breakfast, and totally oblivious of the battle that had just been fought. I found myself, as usual, back with the calves to whom I could reveal the depths of my sadness. I could have a good greet and talk of my hatred until it shrank away completely. I could be totally honest. And I was able to see in their dark eyes, fringed with the most beautiful eyelashes in the whole world, that they completely understood and sympathised.

To this day I refuse to eat veal.

Sylvia Hays

View of Coanda

I warmed to the Coanda Effect,
the idea of it. It is this:
you have a symmetrical set-up,
a cone, a narrow jet, a gas.
You force the gas up through
the jet into the cone.
You wait.
Over time, the gas deviates,
chooses one side of the cone,
rises twirling against the glass.
I love the idea of symmetry,
deviation, a twisted torso,
a laboratory landscape
reaching to the horizon.

Farmhouse B&B

Near darkness brought our footfalls
soft on black soil. Behind the farmhouse
clouds of trees dispersed, unpeeled
a shape of land we couldn't see.
A pool of fallen sky was in its midst.

Suspended from the farther bank by
cloven hooves, a herd of cows,
a thicket of legs, their bodies drowned in silver.

One Angus sat
embedded in land like beaten felt,
an animal warmth
more sensed than seen.

A chill slide of air
shimmered and shook the mirror,
wavered legs, dissolved bodies,
and we drew breath again.

Becky Ford

Left behind

'I want Pink Ted.'

I can't have him left behind, I want Dad to turn the car round and go back, but he won't. He says it's too late and I'll have to manage without him until I get home.

'It was your choice; you wanted to take a different toy. You've got your Andrex puppy instead. You can tell Pink Ted all about it when you get home. He'll be waiting for you when you get back.'

They don't understand; I made a mistake, I was being horrible, I didn't know it would feel like this. Pink Ted will never forgive me – he'll be sad and lonely. I left him lying on the bedroom floor while I put the silly Andrex puppy in my bag instead. The Andrex puppy is new and has soft velvet pads on his paws. Mum sent for him and he came in the post, one for my brother too. We helped cut out the special tokens from the toilet roll packets. When the big envelope came I thought there couldn't be two puppies in it, but they came out all squashed together – they're both the same, but mine's better. My brother has been sucking the ears of his one and already it looks matted and dirty; mine's still soft and fluffy but it doesn't have a name, it's just a toy, something to show Nan. Now I know that's what's wrong.

'I miss Pink Ted!'

'Well, you'll just have to get along without him. You should have thought about this before you threw him out of your bag. I did ask you if you were sure you didn't want to take him.'

But I didn't know then. Mum doesn't understand. I thought she wanted me to be grown up and not always taking Pink Ted everywhere with me like a baby. This holiday I wanted to be different, I wouldn't take boring old Pink Ted, who wasn't even pink any more he'd been washed so often. I'd take my fluffy new puppy and then my brother and I would be the same. But mine would be better cause I'm older and don't need to suck toys like a baby.

I wonder what Pink Ted is doing. There's a horrible frightened feeling in my tummy when I think about him at home in my bedroom on the floor by my bed. The house will be quiet and he'll know I've left him behind, he'll know I've gone on holiday to see Nan without him. It's all my fault.

At first I thought Dad would go back, that they would understand that I had made a mistake – I couldn't go on holiday without Pink Ted. But when I saw the motorway signs I knew it was too late to go back.

'We're nearly in Liverpool now – look, you can't have missed Pink Ted that much if you've only just decided you want him.'

I had been thinking about arriving at Nan's, about climbing up the stairs to the little bedroom, about seeing Big Ted and Sailor Boy and then I realised – they would be expecting Pink Ted, and where was he? How could I tell them I had left him behind? It wouldn't be the same without him.

'I don't want to go on holiday, I want to go home. I miss Pink Ted!'

I am really crying, I can feel my nose dripping. Mum is saying stuff to make me stop. I stare out of the window into the dark and the millions of lights. I usually like this bit of the journey best, trying to recognise where we are, guessing how much longer it will be until I see Nan's road and her house – 85 Rudyard Road. But now I don't want to arrive, everything is ruined and it's all my fault. I don't look at the lights any more, I look at my reflection in the window. I make everything go blurry with my tears. Maybe because I am sorry everything will be all right, maybe it's all a mistake, maybe if I look in my bag again, right at the bottom, Pink Ted will be there after all. Maybe I didn't really take him out, maybe Mum put him back in when I wasn't looking. She knew how upset I would be and so she had brought him in her own bag – she just wants me to know it was wrong to leave him, but now that I'm really sorry she'll get him out.

'Mum, have you got Pink Ted?'

'Pink Ted is where you left him when you threw him out of your bag. Now stop being silly, you wanted to be a grown-up girl and you said you didn't want Pink Ted. What will Nan think if you arrive all upset and crying? We're nearly there!'

I will never leave Pink Ted again.

Ultrasound

It should have been the day we met you
but you had gone,
too quick to be caught on camera.
In the empty space I'd made for you, I saw the future
change before my eyes.
You had never been there
yet your absence sent out waves
through days and months -
dates marking nothing but signifying all
and they will come and find me in the quiet moments.

We talk about the future cautiously
placing ourselves in days that once were yours,
and now must be reclaimed
each day a marker on a journey never made
a chance to rewrite history
but yours is a story which is all beginnings
the end too sad for words to hold.

Stone

The sea had left it for me,
against the wet sand,
a pale promise
In my hand its weight surprises me
but it fits my palm
and my fingers know its curves
I trace a vein of quartz
a lifeline
feel it warm at my touch
my search
I write its message in the sand,
words left for sea and silence.

Alistair Peebles

Bad Call / Good Cop

Five of us in the elevator,
four hip-heavy cops
and me.
A short ride to the fourth floor.

We'd just go see
if it all checked out,
what I'd stammered
at the desk

when it clicked –
'well someone here called in' –
what I'd done:
got the code wrong, dialled 911.

'I was calling for a doctor.
My wife's fallen sick.
Got all muddled up,
I came down here…we're in 406…

'The clerk was trying to help me
get an outside line…'
A long look.
'Can you show us, please?'

———

We squeeze along the corridor,
find no aftermath, of course.
Nothing like. No Barton
Fink-type mayhem,

only Carol, paler now,
whispering, 'what'd they say?'
'They'll send someone
if we ask: $250 on the nail.'

But the cops conferred.
No call-out doctor'd
have the drugs right there,
this time of night.

And they offered us a ride,
which we took,
rode the cold steel bench
four blocks to St Vincent's.

Alison Flett

Charlotte (extract from a novel in progress)

Well I'm not one for all the celebrations anyway, the ran-dan of it all, the stramash. It's a waste of time if you ask me, really, what is there to celebrate? Oh I had everything as clean as I could for the bells of course, that's one thing I always do. After all, if the house isn't clean when you bring the year in, it will stay dirty for the remainder of it. But with the three of them here, great lummocks that they are, nothing stays clean for long. They have no idea, really they don't, the bother they put me to with their mank and midden that they clart through the house on shoes and clothes and hands. They surely think the place cleans itself, the way they take all my effort for granted.

They were all for me coming out tonight, come out and enjoy yourself, they said, as if I'd the time to do that. Right enough it's the 1st of January but that doesn't mean there aren't chores to do. There's routines to be kept to and if you let them slip, well, you lose control then, don't you? The shoes for example. I'm not that fastidious to do them every night but I like to scrub the soles at least once a week. Imagine the germs and muck that would be carted round the house if I didn't! Different if they always took them off inside the door as I've asked them to, but several are the times I've caught one or other of them nipping back in for something they've forgotten without removing their shoes at all.

I've got the six pairs lined up on newspaper on the bathroom floor. The good shoes and the walking boots. They've their trainers on of course, so I can't do those till the morn. I take out the green plastic scrubbing brush, the one I use for the shoes, and I put on my flock-lined Marigolds. I kneel by the side of the bath and I lift the shoes one at a time into the bath and I scrub at the soles with the soap-caked brush.

Moothless, Handless and Witless I call them, my three trials of labour. Even as they entered the world they were a trial to me, those three boys, and doubtless they will be till the end. Most mothers can look forward to the day when their children leave home but not me, no, not me. They'll be here with me till the day I die, for they'd never manage on their own. My mother couldn't be with me when they were born for she had the twins to look after at home, so I sweated and skrecked my way through the labour alone. Alone but for the midwives who had little sympathy, the understanding being that I had brought it on myself. And in fact this is a truth I cannot deny for it was my own foolishness that led to their conception. I was a bright lass, the dux of the school and set for the university, but I threw it all away on a whim.

I begin to rinse the shoes, running water from the shower head over the soles, taking care not to let it run onto the leather. Grey soap scum swirls about the plughole, sucked down clockwise, draining away into the pipes that run beneath the house, across the rocky shoreline, and out into the sea.

My father went to sea when he was still a boy, ran away on a cargo ship at the age of fourteen. He lay awake in his bed one night and he heard my granny and granda discussing his future; he was to take an apprenticeship at the bakery, a safe secure job. My father didn't want to be a baker for he loved the sea with the blood and bones of him and he longed to live in the midst of it, floating on a boat with the water all about him. He climbed out of his bedroom window that same night, down the side of the house and away down to the pier where a tall creaking sailing ship, filled with sheepskins and salted beef, strained at ropes in the harbour. They signed him up as a cabin boy and he never came home for six years, my granny and granda only getting word of him from other sailors who had seen him in this port or that.

It was my mother kept my father at home in the end. He was tall, my father, over six foot, with a shock of dark hair and dancing eyes and long, gentle fingers. This was how he won my mother who came from the grand house on the hill and was bonny and rich and could have had her pick of men. All her riches and her relations with her family were cut off when she and my father were married, but she was happy with him, for the most part, I think she was. She learnt to cook and bake and clean, though she'd never had to do those things before. And she abided by all the sailor superstitions though she secretly laughed at them. Never put your spoon through the shell of your boiled egg. A whistling woman is bad luck. Never throw stones into the sea. Throw salt over your left shoulder if you spill it. It was a dangerous thing, to live or work on the sea, you never knew when it might come for you. Watching out for the little things though, that helped. It helped you feel in control.

When we all lived on Muckle Isle and my father worked on the ferry, taking folk to and from Peedie Isle, my mother would rise early with him to bake bannocks. My father would set off for the harbour, to get the boat ready for sailing, and later my mother would run after him with warm floury bannocks wrapped in a checked teacloth, enough for all the crew. There was one time I mind my mother tying on a headsquare and running off with the warm bannocks claucht against her chest and her floured pinny flapping in the wind. I waited at the window till I saw her come back up the close with the empty cloth flickering in her hand and laughter dancing in her eyes. Oh me, she said, there's some commotion on the pier today alright, what a rammy, what a rammy! and she laughed. Thirteen ministers there were, all in long black cloaks with the white collars, milling about on the pier like black backed gulls, squawking and complaining and trying to get on the ferry, and the crew of the ferry were off the boat and shaking their heads and arms waving and all in a right state. There was to be a new minister on Peedie Isle and the others were wanting to go over for the induction, but it was bad luck to cross the sea with a minister on board and with thirteen of them, thirteen! There was no fear of the ferry sailing with thirteen ministers! Eventually it was agreed that if the ministers went and got changed, took off their black robes and donned civic garb, they could cross to the island. But it was an ill thing to do, to try and trick the powers that be, for they see all and are not to be fooled by what you dress it up in. A fortnight later, the engineer Jimmuck's wife lost her bairn and the following week my own father slipped on the deck and broke his arm and was away from the boat for a month while it healed and no pay, nothing coming into the house. That's what happens when you try to trick fate.

I shake as much water as I can from the shoes and I place them back on the newspaper beside me. I turn on the shower and skoosh it around the bath, rinsing it all down, making sure all the water from the shoes has run away down the plughole. I rinse the scrubbing brush too and put it away in the box under the sink and I get out the bottle of Cif lemonfresh and the toothbrush for the taps. I squeeze Cif onto the toothbrush and I use it to clean around the taps, right into all the crevices and up inside the spouts, amazing the black gunk that collects in places you don't expect, places you can't see.

Even though they came from out of my own self, they were like strangers to me, those three boys. They don't look like me, they're like him, with their red hair and their fair skin. The first to come out of me was Moothless, a door, doun-lookin bairn from the start. Magnus he was christened but he was aye Moothless to me and he fairly gave me the creeps the way his pale blue eyes followed me about the room and never a peep out of him. Folk thought him a contented soul for he never gret, but he never laughed either, nor even smiled. He just watched, always watched with those eyes of his, lingering softly on everything they touched like they were eating what they saw. Gads!

Then there was Handless, though I called him Fergus for long enough, till his clumsiness became apparent. What a handless cratur indeed. He was forever dropping, breaking, cowping over anything that came in his path. He was not allowed to set the table in the end, for the amount of plates and saucers and cups he dropped and broke. He could never ride a bike, still can't and his brothers take turns shaving him for he can't manage that either. Even his words are all mixed up.

When in the shop -

are you needing milk -

is what Janice asked me -

he will say, and though I've come to understand his patchwork speech it irks me still, it does irk me.

And then on the heels of Handless came Witless and he was a daftie from the beginning having not even the wit to be born the right way up. He was breech and there was thought he might not make it but he did after all, though maybe he lost some oxygen and that was the cause of his daftness. He made noise enough alright but what a noise, and that glaikit expression. Oh he was cheerful too was Angus, not like Moothless, but daft as a brush and what a dither. I ken a mother's meant to love her bairns come what may but I'll tell you the truth, I never could, not really. I never did harm by them, though often enough I wanted to. They were fed and clothed, kept clean and dry, but they didn't make my heart sing the way they were supposed to. No, they never did that.

I put more Cif on the toothbrush and use it on the basin taps. Then I take the shower and rinse off first the bath, then the basin. Finally I rinse off the toothbrush and put it away under the sink. I take out one of the new J-cloths and use it to wipe down the taps, the bath and the basin, wiping away all the water drops so that everything shines again. I feel better after that, my little jobs all done, order restored. I can relax.

I liked him fine enough, he worked on the boat with my father and I'd kent him nearly all of my life. Always he wore a hat, a knitted woollen one that covered his hair, for redheads were bad luck at sea. He liked books, which was more than the boys my own age did, all just interested in the one thing. We spoke a lot about books and he lent me many. Good stuff, not the rubbish they had in the library. Tolstoy and Dickens and Hemingway. I would read them and we would speak about them afterwards. My father laughed at us. The bookworms he would call us. Sometimes we would go for a walk and a talk though my father wasn't so keen on that. He's old enough to be your father, he would say. What's he wanting to go out walking with you for? We went out anyway, though it had to be a secret after that. One night he took my hand as we were walking and that had to be a secret too, though I didn't mind it at all, not really. The kissing was different, I wasn't so sure, but I never stopped him for I was fond of him and he was a friend of my father's besides. It was only the once that he took it further and I did try, to begin with, to make him stop, to stop his big rough hands from pulling at my clothes, bumfling up my skirt. But then it hardly seemed worth it, all that struggling, and it was over soon enough. I saw him less after that. He never brought any more books. He still came round the house sometimes, after work with my father, but we didn't go for any more walks. It was the books I missed the most. And the talking about them.

When I began to show, no-one ever asked about the father. I was given plenty abuse for the state I had gotten myself into but as to the man involved, that question was never put to me. And even afterwards, with the three of them that like him and him being a twin himself, still his name was never mentioned. Always it was assumed that I had been responsible, that I had let everyone down with my dreadful behaviour, and I suppose I believed that myself.

I carry the shoes back through to the porch and I line them up on the shoe rack. Then I go back to the bathroom for the newspaper. I'll get off to my bed now, back to my book, *Anna Karenina* it is. It's a book I love, there's so much in it. It's the third time I've read it and I feel I could read it again and again and still not see everything there is to see. If there was someone I could speak to about it, that would be the thing, then it would be easier to make sense out of it all. We all need someone, don't we?

Someone to share things with, someone whose hand we can hold in the darkness, someone to help us make sense of our lives. One mistake I made and I forfeited all of that. One mistake. Sure it was my own fault, I'm not denying that but it irks me still, it does irk me.

Dorrie Morrison

Old Age

Old Age
comes
slowly.
Creeping.
Stealthily –
stealing.

Please –
Old Age
don't
steal all
my sense of delight.

Then and now

Then
us
we
ours
together.

Now
I
us
mine
alone.

Finality

A
heart
stopped
beating.

A
man
died.

Past
tense
began.

Bill Wilson

Jake, a character study

I met Jake, not his real name, some years ago in Glasgow. He had a poor start in life, yet despite that, or, because of it, he developed into a sharp, streetwise character, able to look after himself, a product of this city.

Before he was born, his promiscuous mother ended up on the streets. With no home, and sleeping rough, it was all downhill for her until she was found one night by a charity worker, dirty, starving - and pregnant. Taken into care, where she had food, and shelter, she prospered. On recovering from the birth, accommodation was found for her, and Jake was fostered. He has not seen her since. He never knew his father.

Cautious with people he does not know, he can however, make himself agreeable in company, particularly when it is to his advantage. However, with his 'ain kind' he can quickly take offence, get aggressive, and fight. Strongly built, by getting his retaliation in first, he often sees off his opponent. Even these victories are at a cost, leaving him bruised and bleeding. One would think that, particularly as he gets older, common sense would prevail, but that is lacking in his make up. He lives by the Glasgow 'Prodie's' call, 'No Surrender!'

By contrast, he is interested in birds - no, not the Glasgow 'burds', but real birds that fly. Bird-watching demands patience, and he seems to have acquired that. Although fidgety and easily distracted at other times, when settled down to study birds, he can sit still and quietly concentrate. Over the years he has developed an impressive understanding of birds and their habits. Once, when visiting me in my home outside Glasgow, he brought an injured bird in from the garden. Identified as a collared dove, it was a beautiful bird, but too badly injured to survive.

I still see him from time to time. There he is now at the back door.

Yes, tidying himself up before he comes in, he is enthusiastically washing his face, and less accessible parts of his anatomy as he carries out his ablutions with remarkable feline dexterity.

With the sun shining on his fur, he is a fine figure of a tabby cat, real name Tennicker, the name I gave him on giving a ten pound donation to the Cat Protection League, whence he came.

Ian McDonough

Air Born

A thing has ripped the sky, weighted
like a stunt kite free of wind.
Crumpled, half-conscious on the beach,
ears leaking sea-green blood,
it rolls its cloudy eyes,
voices a note like a whalebone flute.

Men arrive and nail the carcass to a board.
Crossing themselves, muttering,
glowering at its feathers, fingers, toes,
they haul it up the harbour hill.
The man-gull clears its throat,
sings of its death in measured, courtly tones.

It sings of tar, Deuteronomy, arithmetic,
the gloriousness of birds, the ghastliness of man.
Secrets rise like Titans from the village green
till, crazed, the humans stuff its mouth with rags.
The gull sings on as flocks of villagers are drawn
to feel the sharp relief of salt on open wounds.

Children start to itch and agitate their skin,
grin widely when white feathers bloom on limbs.
As the wind lifts they beat their arms together,
fly swift and strong beyond the silly village.
Far below the humans cast up unbelieving eyes
towards the air's unparalleled geometry.

Fiona MacInnes

The art of grown-up lying

If life could be a Mondrian it would be full of orange squares, crisp black lines and perfect edges. Sometimes though it might not be so perfect, be a bit scummy and have to be a Ben Nicholson with dirty beige circles, a thin line and a magnolia crescent.

There is no start to these things, only a kind of osmosis and you wake up in a different place. Something has changed and then it's really a bit of a surprise. There is no need to tell anyone about it. The change can be a silent thing. It makes it more precious.

The less people know the better. It doesn't need to have a plan. Keeping to plans is always difficult. Sticking to something already thought up is difficult too. It's better to find yourself in the middle of it. It's like getting a start without knowing it.

Getting a lift off with denial.

See Allison, she was there. The person making up the commentary in her head proclaimed it, *A grand production in the theatre of her life*. Critics might later say she was *immersed in the drama of denial in the dead end of minimalism*. But right then she didn't care because she was the star even though nobody knew it yet.

By the time they find out it's really me, I will be so good at this role that I will be completely convincing.

And so she will. People will be amazed. They will be shocked and amazed. There will be accolades. Exclamations. Joy. The world will change and no one will believe it was just her all along.

Already it's easy, and it works!

Of course she wasn't thinking about it at all to start with. There was too much else on to fend off. Things to manage, compartmentalise. She got up in the morning, like she had always done since she was a little girl, without question. No skiving school, you coped through thick and thin. She walked about, did what she was told, was a good girl and practised the piano. University material without a doubt they nodded conspiratorially.

At first there was no obvious difference. She found she could shut her face down and just look out from the eyes. Most people were too stupid to notice any change.

Too much communication can be a bad thing. You can lose control that way.

All that indiscriminate smiling.

So liberating to discover how easy it was to lie. After all these years of rigid truth, lying came as a happy release. The commentator was giving advice to liars – *it's best to be grown up about your lying. Select your lies for the situations that most require it. Sometimes you can indulge in reckless lying just for a laugh. But you can only do that very occasionally, or it diminishes the important lies*.

'How are you?'

'Fine.'

It kept her going thinking how shocked people would be when they realised. The big surprise she was planning for them. She would smirk to herself in her bedroom. Sometimes laugh when she thought how stupid they all were and how clever she was.

The osmosis crept in over the top of the numbness – a slowly solidifying resin covering the broken skelfs in her head and trapping them forever. Those other things – denied formation into words and thoughts that would go away if you found a secure enough box to put them in.

She couldn't cry. Crying was like a beginner's emotion. It didn't merit the situation. It was like toy sadness. *Pathetic.*

She never cried about things. She was just stunned gradually by that numbness like everything was shut. No feeling, no sadness, no anger, no nothing.

It was like a kind of trance and then she got used to it and it really became quite comfortable.

And then she couldn't feel anything.

She took a ring pull from a can of Pepsi and scored it across her forearm. Not once, but a whole lot of times. She didn't do the wrists. The trance hadn't taken her there yet.

The scoring was just so that she could feel the soreness. Remember what *feeling sore* was like. See the blood and then know that she was hurt. It was just that she wasn't sure what hurt felt like any more. It was much clearer if you could see blood.

She got to love the lying.

Deception was a joyous and special way of life. Banging around the kitchen making cakes and bread and scones. Huge plate-loads of hot pancakes covered with a clean dish towel from the drawer in the oak chest of drawers. The collection of brothers and sisters and their friends crowded round the table, all gazing up like the adoring at the last supper as she took the hot scones from the oven.

The smell was always intoxicating, and she would put them down in the middle of the table while there was a commotion to find knives. She could eat the smell and would turn away to get butter and jam from the cupboard. Get lost in making the coffee. Appear busy. Become invisible. It was all a success if no one saw that she hadn't eaten a single one.

'Oh I'm sick of looking at all that food. I ate a heap of it while I was baking.'

A single circular pancake could be used to authenticate the act if required. There was always a contingency to divert suspicion. The longer she kept up the deception the better she felt.

'Wow, Allison. You look amazing. You've lost weight. You look great.'

'Have I? God knows how that's happened. I've been eating like a horse.'

Life was always breakfast, dinner and tea
breakfast dinner and tea
breakfast dinner and tea

'Second helping, dear? Will you finish this off, I want to get the pot cleaned?'

Then one day it was two bags of cheese and onion crisps and a can of lager.

And that was for dinner. Or an approximation. Not even at the right time. But at that part in the sentence admittedly.

She kept the sequence in her act. Some routines were necessary. Stage managed concessions.

No meat, no tatties.

'I've had my dinner already.'

And after that it was easy.

She watched forkfuls of mashed potatoes being shovelled into mouths, pie crusts dripping with gravy, knives corralling carrots and peas into manageable situations. Mouths smeared and ungainly in actions of chewing, swallowing. The ugliness of it all. Breughel's common people.

Observing like a chronicler standing above it all. By now she was safely cocooned away from contamination. Only sometimes she was a little tense that she might be discovered.

'I've gone off meat. I'll just have an apple.'

Privately she was elated. She locked herself in the bathroom and got on the scales. Not every day. Only once a week. There had to be some treats.

The weighing became a ritual. She waited for it. Denied herself a quick hop although the scales leered at her. That way she could be sure there would be some difference. A reason for joy, private success. There always was.

The eight stone marker came into view and the needle crept steadily towards it. Then past it heading for the seven. It was sheer happiness. She went out and bought a pair of boys' Wranglers with 30-inch hips.

A landmark.

It got easier and easier.

Breakfast was easy. You could stand against the sink and hug a mug of black coffee, when all the other seats were taken and there was no room at the table. No use squandering unnecessary calories by adding milk, when no one could see what you were drinking anyway.

'I'm never hungry in the morning. It's too early for me to eat.'

It was like discovering a new person, letting the bones come to the surface. Going to bed early with the steady hunger a constant undertone.

Had to be subdued.

Forcing sleep to nullify it.

Lying on her back because the hip bones ground the mattress. Red weals in the morning.

Wonderful flat stomach.

Then concave stomach. Rounding inwards like the inside of a bowl. That gentle valley between the rib cage and the hip bones. That's what glaciers did.

Soft valleys.

Bed sores.

Vodka doesn't count as food.

When she thought about it there was a huge imbalance in what went in and what came out. There would have to be extra account taken of that to get the ratios equal. All these years of taking in too much and not being careful to ensure it was all expelled. Simple maths really. The balance would have to run the other way now. To make sure things were evened up. The ledger.

And the problem of Valerie's wedding. There was no way out of it. The three-course meal and starters and cheese and puddings with wedding cake and everything, had to be eaten. It was going to be too difficult to properly avoid detection.

The prospect could have been really scary. The possibility of the scales going the other way. Meaning something else had taken control of her. She had a new plan but if the new plan didn't work there would have to be a fast for a whole week as punishment.

After all that careful work and planning. Thinking ahead. Winning. It wasn't all going to waste now. And anyway it wasn't finished. The transformation was incomplete.

She made sure all the other toilet cubicles were empty before she started. And it was easy too. It was such a relief. Putting her fingers into the back of her mouth. Further than she'd ever put them before. Her whole fist in her mouth. Feeling for the back of her tongue, the tiny retches at first and then the big one. Pulling her hand out in time. Her face red, eyes bleary. Standing over the toilet in her Laura Ashley dress. Sloshing cold water on her face to take the redness away. Dabbing her face with a paper towel. Like being born again.

Going back in for the second course, and feeling really good that now she didn't have to worry about eating any more. There was another way out.

Masticating her way through the cheesecake. She even went back for another helping of Black Forest gateau with cherries. This time she drank a bit more wine to lubricate her gullet.

All these new skills being learned for her secret life.

'Glad to see you're enjoying your food. I thought you were getting a bit too thin.'

Smiling Allison with her deepening eye sockets and everybody fooled. Relief and elation. Her private ecstasy.

A major achievement under her belt at last. Something really meaningful. Precious like gold. Her very own.

Knowing she couldn't tell anyone or the magic would go.

One precision-cut two-centimetre cube of orange cheddar cheese, a single plain digestive biscuit and two quarters of an apple, Macintosh Red

of course.
     A cup of black coffee strategically placed.
     That is all you need to be in control. Ran the commentator.
     And a left forearm, bleeding like a Jackson Pollock.

A week to die

There were big deep baas
like an old smoker
from the far end of the shed
corrugated sheeting resounding
she got propped up on a bale
the back legs would scramble a little
balance then sag
moving her out of the warm skitter
onto clean straw
with offerings of ewe nuts and hay
vitamin injections and water
she sat like a foundered ship
slowly leaking

Alex Ashman

Haiku in a Dundee park

Broken tree branches,
dew hangs still from fir and leaf
tugging heart, lost hope.

Palm to bark it's warm
slow familiarity,
green light fills my eyes.

Under high sweeping trunk,
canopy shades me from sight.
Low, dark, silent world.

Trees fingers drip rain,
in the gloom I lift my face,
a drop hits my cheek.

Emerging in cloud,
wet leaves, thinking of home,
talking to myself.

I reach the road's end.
Endless moment - I break it
choosing my own path.

Lynn Johnson

Becca's Dream
(extract from a novel in progress, *Finding Ginnie*)

It's so cold! A bell drumming in the long, draughty corridor outside the room awakens us and I am glad to leave the uncomfortable, narrow bed with its coarse, thin blanket. With hands that will not work I pull on all the clothes folded in the small wooden cupboard beside the bed, yet still I am chilled to the bone.

The room is full of girls younger and older than me. Trying to dress quickly, some fall in the darkness between the two gas lamps at each end of the long room. Waves of panic ebb and flow as my eyes become accustomed to the dim light. Where am I? The room is familiar but I recognise no one. Three of the older girls are dressing the youngest children.

Be quick otherwise you won't get no breakfast, someone shouts.

Two girls sneeze heavily and I thrust my hands over my ears to shut out the racking coughs around me.

Stop coughing 'cause you won't get no medicine today.

I want to give something to the little girl with the large, frightened blue eyes, but the coldness dulls my brain and I do nothing. The water for washing is stone cold and we hardly tap our faces with it, whilst the stench of the bucket in the corner grows as each girl relieves herself without embarrassment.

Your turn to empty the bucket today someone says to me. After breakfast you can do it. I feel sick as I squat on the bucket, my face burning.

Twenty pairs of shuffling feet stumble towards the hall where we will eat our breakfast. We are too tired to talk.

Through one of the three windows groups of men emerge from a doorway in the building across the yard.

He must be there.

I run to the window but I can't see my father. I haven't seen him for ages. I hope he's alright.

You won't see 'im. Me dad died an no-one told me fer days, said a girl standing next to me.

How will I bear it if that happens?

You got a mum?

'Course I've got a mum.

Then, I see him, head swinging from side to side. He's looking for me! I bang my fist on the window. He hasn't seen me!

Dad, Dad, my voice fills my head, my whole world. But I can't breathe. Am I drowning? The window fogs up as I expel the trapped air and my burning forehead meets the cold glass. Desperately I wipe it with my arm, but it just gets worse and worse. I bang on the window again but he still can't hear me. I scream and scream at him but even as the words leave my mouth, they are lost as the voices around grow louder. He disappears through a door, and is gone.

Daddy! Daddy, I'm here. Look at me!

Arms surround me, pulling me away from the window and I twist and turn, fighting as hard as I can, gripping the sill, but my fingers are slipping away ....

Becca woke with a start, struggling against the arms holding her tightly.

'GET OFF ME. GO AWAY! I WANT MY DADDY!'

'Becca! BECCA!' Kate shook her gently and slowly, Becca's wild eyes focused.

'Mum! Oh, Mum!'

She breathed in short sharp pants and threw her arms around Kate. She was sitting on the pillow now with a rapid pounding in her ears. Kate switched on the bedside lamp flooding the room with light. Becca's relief was audible as she recognised the familiar warm teak furniture of her bedroom, the white rocking chair with the huge teddy she'd won when she was nine, and even the pile of dirty clothes that had not made it into the linen basket.

Shuddering violently, she swallowed several times trying to regain control of her wildly beating heart. Rubbing her eyes, she was surprised to feel the wetness of tears. She took a gulp of water and slid her knees up to her chin hugging them tightly.

What a dream! Where had it all come from? She had been really frightened and even though the aching isolation she had felt on waking had eased a little, she was still trembling and breathing hard.

'Whatever's the matter Becca? You were shouting. Did you have a nightmare, love?'

Kate stroked her hair gently.

'Is she okay Mum?' Daniel appeared in the doorway, scratching the top of his head.

'I'm…I think I'm all right. I had a nightmare. That's all.'

'Jesus, Becca! It must have been a hell of a dream. You were screaming! I thought someone had broken in and tried to kidnap you at the very least. Maybe it was the bogey men,' he said in a creepy deep voice, grinning at her discomfort.

'Now then Daniel, get off to bed. There's no point in frightening her any more.'

Daniel wandered off and Kate turned back to her.

'Want to tell me about it?'

Becca shook her head and then changed her mind, feeling stronger now that Kate was there, her face full of concern.

'It was awful Mum. It was the workhouse!'

'The workhouse?'

'Yeah, you know that place we went to see? You said your granny lived there in the olden days?'

'Well, yes. I know where you mean. You say you were dreaming about it?'

'Yes, I dreamed I was in the workhouse. I'd just woken up, so I must have been living there. We were going to have breakfast. There were lots of girls in the bedroom. Then, I was walking down this long corridor. I looked out of a window and Dad was outside – only it wasn't Dad. It was somebody else, but he was my father. So I banged on the window, and shouted, but he couldn't hear me. No matter how hard I tried, I couldn't make him hear. Then they dragged me away and I woke up. It felt so real, Mum. I was there, at Haddon House, just like your Granny!'

Kate's eyes widened.

'No love, it was a dream, just a dream.'

'It was so cold. I couldn't get warm.' Becca carried on, rubbing her hands up and down her arms, trying to warm them. 'There was no fire and I had to wash in cold water. It was freezing cold and,' she said, shivering again, 'it was one of the rooms we went into. I recognised it. Truly I did.' She stared earnestly at Kate, willing her mother to believe her.

'Well half the duvet was on the floor when I came in. It's no wonder you were cold! Still, it was only a dream. That's all. Feeling better now?'

'Yeah, I think so.'

'If I'd have thought it would give you nightmares, I would never have taken you to see the workhouse. Whatever made you dream about that? Have you been thinking about it?

'No!' She lied.

'Were you worrying about it? You didn't seem too bothered when we were walking around. Did it upset you?'

'I don't think so. I suppose I must have been thinking about it. I would like to find out more about those times. It is interesting when you can see how people were affected by things like that isn't it?'

'Mm, that's why I started looking at it. It's fascinating, but not if it gives you nightmares!' Kate rebuked firmly.

'I'm okay now. Really' said Becca in response to Kate's raised eyebrow.

'Do you think you can go to sleep now?'

'Mm. But leave the light on Mum; I'll switch it off in a few minutes.'

'Sure you're okay?'

Becca nodded and slid down beneath the duvet as Kate quietly closed the door. Left on her own, Becca's thoughts returned to the dream. It was not so vivid in her mind now. The pictures had begun to fade but the feeling of despair and isolation remained with her. Never, in all her life had she felt so unutterably lonely.

This is what Ginnie felt. It came to her suddenly. Her great-grandmother was ten when she was taken into the workhouse, even younger than Becca was now. What must she have felt during those years without her family? Who would have comforted *her* when she had nightmares? She had no-one to tuck her up in bed, to feel her forehead if she complained of a temperature, to comfort her, to listen when she wanted to talk.

Up until now history had not been her favourite subject at school. In fact, she was planning to drop it when she did her A-Levels. But, this was different. She wanted to know more about the children who found themselves imprisoned, for that's what it had felt like to her, locked up in those austere, imposing buildings. Yes, that's what she must do. She would have a look at her mother's family history notes, and then she would do some research of her own. She needed to know what happened to children like Ginnie.

Feeling calmer, she switched off the light and snuggled into her warm, soft bed.

Emma Grieve

The Bridesmaid's Boots

Fairy-tale shoes for an ephemeral princess
satin white and sparkling, an elegant heel;
diamanté echoing the gossamer dress
and dewy beads clinging in the veil.
The perfect shoes for a perfect bride,
but the bridesmaid bargained for boots.

Let the acrid smell rise with the box lid; boots
not graceful or delicate, but shining blue things,
declaring their freshness in bright yellow stitches
and laces auriferous as new-moulded rings.

They are seductively pristine. They tantalise
whilst firmly resisting the unfamiliar feet,
rubbing heels to blooms of callus;
yet with patience and time they gently yield

while satin heels repose unseen,
secreted away after the final dance.
Effulgent and tarnished in one short day,
stored with the memory, and favours, and cards.
But the bridesmaid bargained for boots.

For with warmth the leather is lithe
and faithful to the form of that foot.
More beautiful for its creases and lines, the signs
of wear and experience and use.

Relenting seams, that once mulishly creaked,
now given to hold that familiar shape.
And honed by flaws; they own and are owned,
becoming slippers. Their fit is unique.

Boots; dancing not for a night, but a lifetime
dearer than upon-a-time shoes, and softer.
The bridesmaid bargained for boots
to weather the ever-after.

In response to a Radio 4 programme on GMB

They telt me aboot a man
on the wireless.
They telt me aboot a man that wrote poems
aboot whar I bide, aboot the things I see ivery day.
And the wiy that man githered that things in
and wrapped thum up
in words tae howld the past tae the present,
the present tae the future;
he curled me world in his waarm words.

Bit when they said aboot him,
telt me aboot the pieces and the past,
they didna use me words, or his words.
They used thir words;
pulling out of shape the place names,
rendering the familiar unrecognisable,
distorting the vowels which comfort my mouth.
Twistan at pictyers o' me home.

Fran Flett Hollinrake

Orkney 1974 (extract from a novel in progress)

Marianne lay in bed after James had got up, and stretched her legs as far as they would go, flexing her toes against the wall of the caravan and arching her back. She heard the hiss of the gas ring and then smelt it too, a warm, comforting smell that reminded her of family holidays as a child.

'You want tea?' he called, teaspoons tinkling. Her head ached as she dragged it off the cushion. The window was steamed up and there were puddles of condensation gathering on the metal sills. She dabbed at the water with the nylon curtain, watching the shiny blue material turn dark, then rubbed a small patch of window to peer out. The world, from what she could see, was grey. Misty, dripping, clinging, damp, and relentlessly grey. Marianne pressed her hot cheek to the cold glass and felt her skin tingle. A larger part of the world outside was now visible. A bedraggled duck waddled across the yard, casting around for any tasty titbit that might have risen to the muddy surface. A stream of water fell from the guttering at the edge of the barn into a wooden butt that was already overflowing and creating a stream which was gathering strength as it flowed through the yard.

By now, Marianne had got used to the sound of rain on the tin roof, but last night had been particularly heavy – stair-rods, James called it, and it had woken them up. The baby, unusually, had woken too and they had taken her into the narrow bed, where the three of them had lain wide-eyed, listening to the pounding and roaring above them. James was up early. He wanted to see to the beasts, get them fed and watered and well into their day, because in less than an hour the chosen few would be loaded up into the truck and taken to the Show.

Sipping her tea, Marianne continued to observe the world through a small patch in the misty window. She could hear grunts and snorts and a tin bucket getting knocked over. The door of the stable swung open and James led out a handsome Clydesdale on a leather rein. Her hairy fetlocks had been brushed then carefully tied against her legs to keep them out of the mud. Her mane was beautifully plaited. Ma Matches had been taught a special pattern by her mother and she would have spent a good hour combing and weaving and entwining ribbons in the silky strands. The horse – Bessie? Betsy? Marianne was never sure – snuffled the air and munched on an apple. James murmured something that Marianne could not hear. An endearment or a word of fond encouragement, judging by the look on his face. She felt suddenly like a spy, or an eavesdropper who hears nothing good of themselves. James and the horse walked side by side to the trailer and the huge, graceful animal stepped daintily up the ramp, huffing through her nose as James stroked her cheek.

A movement to her left, and the kitchen door opened. With a sharp bark a collie appeared and bounded towards the door, shaking its coat and anticipating Ma's breakfast whistle. Baby Alexa started to cry. Marianne finished her tea and swung her legs off the bed. One foot met cold bare lino, the other met mud-encrusted matting. She found her slippers – an old pair of Ma's - and suitably shod, crossed to the baby's cot. Alexa was less than six months old but already seemed effortlessly herself. She stared at her mother, stopping in mid-wail, and held out her hand as if in greeting. Marianne met her gaze and shook the little fingers solemnly. 'Good morning Miss Alexa. How are you today?' Alexa winked and blew a bubble. Marianne turned to get another blanket and missed the moment when her baby's beautiful eyes changed from palest blue to a deep shade of violet.

Sally Heddle

Ammonite

Deep in the earth, away from searching eyes
it lay enclosed in fractured rock.
Hard grey stone,
now cracked open.

Our past lies here.
Rays of translucent shell, brittle and sheer
curled, once, to shield its vulnerability:
submarine drifting in murky waters,
wandering across vast prehistoric oceans,
seeking its food.

Are its secrets now revealed?
Only in death do we behold
this delicate interior
this eternal imprint of life.

Wind Farm

They stand erect on barren heath.
Emerging from the morning mist
their whitened spears reach heavenward
to face a bold Quixote,
challenging him anew to tilt and dare.

Has some unknown hand refashioned them?
For harvesting the air,
they reap the wind -
on and on,
steadily round and round,
endlessly grinding the sky.

L.C. Littlejohn

Brief Encounter

March 2001
James Merchant drove his jeep into the village square. Easing himself down to the tarmac, he winced as pain shot through his back. God, he thought, old before my time. At only 42 he felt as if the unrelenting lambing season had added ten years in as many weeks.

Raking his hand through his dark hair, he headed into the village store. At once a neighbouring farmer, Edwin Lamont, bore down on him.

'Have you heard the news, James?'

James looked warily at Edwin who was known to be friendly with the shop owner and village gossip, Mrs Blane.

'I hope it's good, whatever it is,' said James.

'Afraid not. Another farm has got Foot and Mouth…and this time it's even nearer to us. Right at the county border.'

'Oh, my God…' James felt his heart take a dive.

'I know, it's not good news at all.' Even Edwin, who was the nearest thing to what could be called an optimistic farmer, was very down-in-the-mouth.

'I wish you hadn't told me,' said James and left the shop empty-handed.

It was eight o'clock that night when James closed the byre door and sighed. Nothing too disastrous, even the animal he'd worried about this morning seemed to be looking better and eating at last.

The February night was dark and still. He could hear the river nearby. Heavy with the last rains it was rushing on, wide and full. On an impulse he walked through the farm steading and up onto the road. He crossed the dark pathway and gained the bridge that spanned the swollen river. In the light of the moon he could see clearly the banks and the dark, surging body of water between.

Of course, it wasn't just the latest dire news that had made him leave the village shop so abruptly. It was much more than that. This new blow had come at the end of a dreadful year. Foot and Mouth had affected the next county, but not up to the border as now. Every farmer hated the disease. Even if you were one of the lucky ones and your farm was not affected, the loss of sales was crippling. He felt as if he had been working his fingers to the bone for a living that was going to end up in burning, stinking flesh and bone.

And then, just before Christmas, his mother had died. She had always been on the farm; always there in a crisis; always ready to give her advice and her physical help when she could. He missed her every day.

Now James was alone; the disease seemed no nearer its conclusion and he waited daily to hear the dreaded news that his cattle, his beautiful Aberdeen Angus, were to be piled up in pits and burnt. James knew he was lonely and depressed but he seemed not to be able to do anything about it. Life was just a thankless round of work and nothing seemed worthwhile.

James leaned on the bridge parapet and looked down at the rushing river water, dark and deep and cleansing. So easy, so easy…he would not be the first to choose this way. After all there was no one to miss him. He tensed. The bridge moved gently beneath his feet and someone came to lean companionably beside him.

'James. A fine night on the river.'

It was old Ebenezer from the village. At one time he too had farmed, but he had retired into a little cottage in the square.

James nodded hello, not trusting his voice to speak.

'Been a bad year,' said Ebenezer quietly. James felt as if the old man had been inside his own head.

'It's not easy,' the old man continued almost to himself, 'when everything seems to go wrong. You've had a tough time, James.'

'Yes.'

'But never fear. All bad things eventually come to an end and this will too.' The old man spoke with such conviction that James suddenly felt ashamed. The old man patted him on the shoulder and walked quietly away.

Next morning, James felt better. It was an inexplicable. He just knew that the worst was over. The future beckoned and it could be anything he wanted – farming or out of farming, he would make his way.

He drove into the village for early supplies of milk and bread. Mrs

Blane was on the go early in the village shop and bustled about fetching his order.

'You'd have heard about old Ebenezer, James?'

'What about old Ebenezer?'

'Eeh, he died last night. His daughter found him when she went in to get his tea at five o'clock.'

'*Five* o'clock? Surely you're mistaken. He couldn't have died at five o'clock. Why, I just saw him…'

'Yes, his daughter told me herself and in fact I met her coming out of his cottage just after it happened. She was terribly upset.'

Mrs Blane went on, 'I remember Ebenezer well. In fact I think he had a real thing going with your Mam when they were just young things. Both gone now though.'

For the second time in as many days James Merchant left the shop empty-handed.

Olive Ritch

The hand game

Let not thy left hand know
what thy right hand doeth.
And let not your mother
hide their secrets in silence,
for only she knows the stories that lie
in the lines of the palms
of your hands. She knows
but cannot speak the words, tongue-tied.
Slumped in her chair
she takes from your hand
the medicine, three-times daily
and smells your nicotine breath
when you tuck her in at night
before switching off the light. Sometimes
you creep back in and your mother knows
the colour of your filial love
from the tone of the touch
of your Hyde or Jekyll hand.

La Villa

Pensa migliori giorni la villa triste, pensa
young voices filling its empty spaces
with the sound of *The Trout* jumping
scale to scale, aunt Betty mouthing:

pianissimo, pianissimo.
Buttoned up to the neck, she
coaxed her singers higher
and higher, fortissimo.

Sometimes the house sighed,
sometimes shuddered, soprano
voices soaring skywards. At night,

aunt Betty played solo, chromatic chords
planted, growing into something, life
promises draining, pianissimo

(*Pensa migliori giorni la villa triste, pensa -*
The sad villa thinks of better days; it thinks of)

Diana Clay

Tree with many branches

A short walk
from Belcoo to An Blaic
but a long journey.
In the distance lough Mcnean
gleamed in fitful sunlight.
Poetry in three languages
english and gaelic ulster scots:
we strutted our stuff.
Cathal Bui's birthplace
and a tour of
the old stones.
But best was the craic
in the snug at Dolan's:
everyone gave of their own
poetry, fiddle
songs of lament for the land,
the man whose poetry
was about his father
couldn't read it for crying.
In the snug, we understood.

Bill Ferguson

Mum Revisited (extract from a novel in progress)

Disappearing? She wouldn't hear of it.

'You sure?' said Burk. 'I mean I'd understand. Might be a bit of a problem, a bit awkward you know? – me never having met Em and being here… there… you know, "around" at night?'

No-no-no, he wasn't disappearing! It'd be fine. Em'd been told he was Mum's new boyfriend, plus Nicholas was sure to've thrown in his tuppence-worth, seeing as how he was never off the phone to his sister – at *Mum's* expense she might add! – no-no, Em'd be cool abourit, but Weemutt'd need to be placed under bedroom-arrest that'd be the only thing, couldn't have him roaming about the house with the baby around.

So? So the dog'd be sleeping with them, Em and the baby'd be in the spare room, Nicholas in his pit as per usual – easy-peasy see! no problem whatsoever. It was only for a few days. Everything was arranged.

'You'll like Em,' she promised, feeling as if she needed to make amends for Nicholas's brightness not having shown much lately.

They picked her up from the terminal near enough midnight. Mum could tell right away something was up. Her only daughter wasn't comfortable, though what the trouble was was anyone's guess at the minute, maybe just the long trip with the baby who'd kept being sick, but it could've been being a mum herself now or '*Gran* fussing!' or Burk's uneasy presence, or maybe she'd had a barney with whatsizname - Eric the baby's dad, he'd been supposed to've been coming too but hadn't made it. Maybe it was all of the above just brimming up and spilling over, she didn't know.

Whatever it was, Em wasn't herself. But what with getting the buggy and bags and baby out the lift and all the faff unfastening the carrycot out the pram and wedging it so's baby'd face forwards like Em was saying – no, not backwards like Burk was wanting, going on about whiplashes and trains blah blah blah, what the dickens'd that got to do with it! – wedging it, just jamming it like she said between the back of the slid-back front-passenger seat and the backrest of the back seat, *now* not being the right time for instruction on making a car seat out the contraption and belting it in like you should. But anyway, what with all that, and stowing the rucksack and the gutted carcass of the pram in the boot, plus the wind and rain and pitch-blackness that he hadn't even thought to've brought a torch for, *plus* the baby starting to mewl, Mum knew it wasn't the right time to be asking Em what was up.

'It's probably because I'm here,' fretted Burk over the next evening's after-work first cuppas and roll-ups.

'No-no-no,' she shooed, prickling that he'd twigged so soon things were as-you-were Em-wise. 'It's just... I dun-*no* what it is! It's nothing. Don't worry abourit, she's fine.'

Mum didn't want it being an issue. Mum was doing her utmost to be positive look. Mum could do without unhelpful whiffs of negativity right now thank you very much. Her daughter was out-of-sorts, no doudabourit, but Mum had every confidence. Em'd be just fine.

'Maybe it's post-natal depression,' Burk trespassed airily.

She didn't like the sound of that. Checked his face for straightness. Said nothing, not in the mood for having her leg pulled.

'Or is that just another of those phantom yuppie conditions you've been telling me about?' the bigfoot blundered on, straying well off-limits, that annoying grin of his lit-up.

She shot him a look.

'It's nothing,' she cautioned doing po-faced, not-liking-one-bit being made to feel apologetic and *defensive* about family. It was just Eric-the-bastard. He'd not been in touch. Too busy to phone – huh! – too busy down the pub with his mates more like if she knew anything aboudit. Em'd be all right when she settled a bit. Needed a break that's all. Took some getting used to a new baby did, especially your first. She just needed to get out more.

Burk could give Em and the bairn lifts, he rambled. No-no-no, Em could use Jaunty, Mum insisted, wanting her daughter to have the space she needed, wanting her to want motherhood, grieving to see she didn't.

'Why don't you go out for a bit Em? Go for a walk, get some fresh air,' she counselled in the morning, readying herself for work.

'Lissn chiwdrun, Gran's tawkin!'

'Shut it Nicholas! What you doing up anyway?'

'Needid a leak. If thass lyke, awr-oy wif ewe.'

'Fresh air's good for you,' she sniffed, ignoring loudly. 'Baby'll like that.'

'Yeah,' said Em.

'Go over and see Francine, you could… later on… if you fancied.'

'S'pose.'

'Why don't you? Take the car, I don't need it when I'm working, I can walk, use the bike, whatever.'

'Could do.'

'You must go and see Francine while you're here. It'd be a shame to miss her when you've got the chance. You'll have to, look. She's bound to want to see the baby. Must be due herself in a couple of months musn't she?'

'Yeah.'

'How many's she got again? Three is it?'

'Yeah.'

'All girls aren't they?'

'Yeah.'

'They'll be chuffed-to-bits to see a bonny wee boy then, won't they now,' sang Gran, tickling baby's little tum for him.

'I think he's got colic,' said Em.

Colic? Never! Don't be so daft – Gran was sure it was no more than a touch of wind after his feed, she could tell by the way his eyes rolled look, just needed to be burped properly to get rid of it – 'don't he the little darlin,' she crooned through his wooze-zone right into the infant's rolling-eyed blissed-out depth-of-field.

It'd been a grand few days. They'd done the pool after work – baby's first dip. They'd done walkies galore. They'd done nappy-changes and feeds and burpings and puttings-down and liftings-up, bathtimes and bedtimes, nightmares and nightnursings, songs and stories, teddies and toys. They'd goo-gooed and gurgled and trilled to her heart's content.

They were having a great time, teaching by example. Relearning, example by exhausting example, that that was the good thing about grandkids: you could hand them back look!

Almost a week gone and everyone was starting to get a bit narky, getting on each other's nerves they were. Apart from that, what with a houseful of kids and so much going on, they hadn't been able to… you know… So Mum decided to leave the young-uns to it: she and Burk were breaking loose for an adult night at his place.

It went well. *Really* well. It was worth waiting for actually.

What with it being Saturday they'd been volunteered for babysitting so Burk might as well grab fish suppers for the two of them on the way up the road from work. If that was all right she'd checked, never liking to take things for granted.

The kids were doing a meal for themselves, Nicholas in charge of the nosh, tattie-peeler in hand, giving a good impression of having everything under control, Em in her mood, perching herself on a stool and thumbing through a mag soon as she'd handed bairn-duties over to Mum, who'd hardly had time to get her anorak off let alone a cuppa tea or anything look, while there *they* were getting stuck into a bottle of château-neuf de plonk.

She left them to their devisings – steak for braising and tatties that'd mash and swim in onion gravy by the look of it – and tried to chill for half an hour in the front-really-back room next to the sighing carrycotted tot, though she couldn't even have a cig what with the arrangements which'd also mean she and Burk when he came'd have to take it in turns to gatecrash the tea-party cussuf the kitchen being the designated smoking room while that baby was around.

She'd had to show him what to do during the week but Burk was finally getting the hang of holding the bairn, could even give it its bottle which he was doing now, though he couldn't be expected to burp it properly yet. Satisfied she'd got the two of them settled, she candid-snapped them with Digi, saved it what with it being a good one, and finally caught up with her fish supper in the kitchen, famished she was.

'You wanna glahrsa woin Mum?'

An empty stood on the worktop and the cork'd been pulled on a full one. Mouth still working on crispy batter, Mum waved away the offer between fingerlicks.

'What you after then?' she frowned as the last swallow went down and the greasy wrappers got severely scrumpled and clapped into a ball, tossed in the air once-twice-thrice in a juggler's flurry and ricocheted off the orange wall, boinging against the back of the overflown bin. He had to be after something.

Number-Three Son interrupted the washing-up to send a peeved look and an 'Oy only ahrsd if you – lyke – wannid a drink' over his half-turned shoulder.

'I know you Nicholas.'

'You know how we're going out Mum,' Em stepped in.

'Yee-aaas,' rifted Mum.

'We were wondering…'

'Don't like the sound of that!'

'We've only got, like, a fiver between us. Well I've got a fiver'n Nick's got zilch. We were just wondering if you could lend us some money.'

'What happened to your own money?'

'We'll pay you back! I will anyway. My giro's not due til next week, that's all.'

But Mum'd read the script and was already fishing for her wage packet in the depths of her anorak, weighing up with her back to them what she'd netted in an inside-out pocket-lining before revealing the size of the catch.

'Any chance you could make it twenty?' brassed Em soon as she saw the folded tenner.

'Twenty! What you think I am? a blummin goldmine? What you need twenty for?'

'Can't have a night out on a tenner.'

'Fifteen,' she reminded. 'You've got a fiver of your own look.'

'Might have to get a taxi back up the road. If it's raining.'

Another haul, another tenner weighed in, she was in no mood for arguing.

'I need it back mind.'

'I'll give you my ten on Thursday'n Nick'll give you his on Friday. Won't you Nick?'

'Ow yeah,' piped Nicholas with conviction over the drumming of water on the sink-bottom, but sounding a bit out of practice.

'Thanks Mum,' remembered Em.

'And don't let Nicholas get pissed, you know what he's like.'

'Fanks Mum!'

'Yeah-well. Have fun.'

She was sounding a bit rusty herself.

One, half-oneish, the baby fast asleep, no sign of the kids, she finally gave in to yawns and proposed bed. Burk was entrusted with both baccy tins and the remains of their carry-out while she put Moby and Digi's batteries on charge and gave the kitchen a last once-over glance of the night. The kids'd pretty much tidied up for a change but she thought she'd better just put that re-corked half-empty bottle out of harm's way, goodness alone knowing what state Nicholas'd be in by the time they got back.

Ownership of the middle of the bed'd already been claimed. No ceremony, no problem: Mum's ever-ready with a ready remedy, especially for dogs getting too big for their boots. The curled-up bedded-down squatter skited to the bottom of the suddenly sloped-up chuted-down dove-it, Mum's foot's extra bit of encouragement rewarded with a satisfying thud on the carpet. Floored paws paused, scrambled, unscrambled, re-found their partners, leapt bedwards, sword-danced over lumpy four-legged hazards, stood waiting for music but there was none to face so turn-and-a-halfed a dog-tired hot slump into the nest of Mum's knee-crooks.

The sleep switch that normally got flicked to 'off'… or was it 'on'? – she must figure that one out sometime… whatever, it wasn't working and she was just re-running all the possibilities about where they, the kids, might've got to, the pubs closing ages ago, probably finding a party, walking back up the road, how long it took, not this long surely, etcetera and so forth, when she heard the back-really-front door go.

'They'll've had enough,' she whispered.

'They'll probably just get to their beds,' supposed Burk.

'Em'll have to give the baby a feed,' Gran corrected. She'd got one prepared and fridged.

'Mum…?'

'What.'

'You awake?'

'What d'you want Em?'

'Where's my bottle of wine?'

'You've had enough to drink, you don't need any more.'

'Where's my bottle of wine Mum?'

Mum's mum.

'It's my wine Mum. Where is it?'

Mum's staying mum.

'Where have you hidden my bottle of wine Mum?'

'We drank it.'

'No you didn't. Where've you hidden it Mum?'

'I'm not telling you… It's late – look at the time. Go to bed Em.'

'It's not fair Mum, that's my bottle of wine…'

Silence.

'Mum?'

'It's in the cupboard.'

Footsteps. Receding.

'Should keep'em occupied for a while,' she tittered.

'What've you done with it?' conspired Burk.

'Take some finding that will.'

Footsteps. Approaching.

'Which cupboard Mum? I can't find it.'

'Don't shout. You'll wake that baby look… come in…'

'I don't want to come in…'

'Open the door then if you don't want to come in.'

'I don't want to open the door. I just want to know where you've put my bottle of wine…'

Silence.

'Mum…'

Silence.

'Mum. Where's my bottle of wine?'

'I've told you, it's in the cupboard.'

'I've looked in all the cupboards. It's not there.'

Silence.

'Which cupboard Mum?'

'The *cupboard* under the *fucking* sink!'

Silence.

'Thank you Mum.'

They weren't in the mood for discussing pester-power right now on account of that wonky sleep switch having self-sorted.

Laureen Johnson

Flame and Shadow

It wis the fire that did it,
diz it fir me every time.
Aw that flickerin flame
and shadows on the waw
and him wi jist the right voice
– know whit Ah mean? –
makes ye listen
makes ye believe
makes ye ... *shiver*.
And Ah did,
honest t' Goad!
It wis the fire, and him
thegither.
Ah could have sat aw night.

It wisnae as if
Ah hudnae heard things
like this before.
Wee folk like trows
crop up in ither places,
witches and ghosts
walked everywhere
(even in Edinburgh!)
but there's somethin
aboot this *place*.
Maybe it's the wind
moanin
maybe it's the miles
o darkness, total darkness,
maybe it's jist the whisky!

But the stories have a ring to them.
They belong here,
true or no.
And how could they be true?
– the skull an the bridegroom,
Johnnie Mann's Ghost,
and the fiddler o Goard
– aw that!
An whit's aw this
aboot meetin folk
face t'face,
some'dy ye know,
and they dinna speak.
then ye hear they're deid
in some ither place
and ye couldnae have seen them,
ye saw a *feyness*.
Whit's aw that aboot?
That's new tae me.
I mean ... diz that still happen?

Ah well,
like Ah said,
it's a guid story.
It's a brilliant story!
It's the voice, that's the thing.
and the fire,
that's whit diz it
every time.

Treeds: the trap, the network, the spoilt pattern and the silent support

For four voices, in any suitable order

Da place I come fae an da hame I hae
da midder and da faider at I hae,
da age dey are, da wark at's ta be dön
wi nane but me ta dö,
da fock aboot at watches every move,
da duty at I hae,
da tocht I tak,
da look apon a face,
da wye dey need me –
every last thing aboot it ties me here
an naething can be dön, an life gengs by.

Da place I come fae an da hame I hae,
da faimily aroond ta back me up,
an gie a haand, an share ita da wark,
when I'm awa at sea,
da money at I bring ta help dem oot,
da pairt I'm come ta play,
da wark I do,
da wife I'm goin ta hae
anidder winter –
everything's wirkin oot, Guid grant it lests
a saison yet! What better place ta be!

Da place I come fae an da hame I hed
aye lippened mair o me as I could gie.
So what I did wis never guid enyoch,
an things cam oot aa wrang.
I brook da pattern, brook da very treeds,

an brook me midder's hert
or so she said,
da hidmast time I guid
ta try an mend it –
everything's reffled up itae my life

an reddin oot's ower gritt a task for me.

Da place I cam fae an da place I bide,
da fock I never towt aboot afore
at cam aroond ta help me at da time
I needed it da maest,
da wark dey shared, da things dey did for me.
Dey kerried me alang
da warst o gaets
until I cam at I
could geng unaided –
everything at dey did I'll never ken
but owe dem mair as wirds could ever say.

---

reffled: *tangled*

reddin oot: *untangling, sorting out*

gaets: *pathways*

Part two

Short pieces generated at
writing workshops in 2007

Roderick Thorne

Tic tacs

Forty-seven misshapen miniature alabaster snowmen
Jumbled in a toy transparent plastic mausoleum.

Fifty-pence piece

This tuppenny-halfpenny coin was once substantial
and looked as though it might be worth two-and-six.

S usie suffered sunburn
H elen hated heat
A lison adored adoration
D octor Davidson directed
E nergy efficient efficacious
S unfree Suntan Salon'.

Kate Townsend

The dog should have answered.
An unnecessary waste
evidenced by the road – red.

Frances Bell

Was it you I found so long ago, shining by that ocean of my childhood, when all seemed boundless rapture? And now I find you in a cardboard box, long-forgotten between the rafters of this house. So glad I am to hold you once again and am so warmed by those memories that had for so many years forsaken me.

S o long old friend
T omorrow will come
O n another rainbow's arc
N ever doubt it
E ven the sun don't shine

Sinclair Scott

The green bowl

The green bowl exploded. Shards of glass spread across the stone floor.
Complete silence reigned. The parents stared aghast at the culprit.
The old lady – more shattered than the glass – sank white-faced to her
chair.
Two hundred years without a scratch
demolished in a second.
The bairn gurgled happily, untouched and unconcerned.
But the heirloom was no more.

The green bowl – haiku

The bowl burst
green shards spread on stone.
Shattered, she stared
her old heirloom gone.

Dave Linklater

St Magnus Cathedral – haiku

Sandstone shelter
centuries sunlit
time out within
traffic outside.

Helga Tulloch

Haiku from two Norman MacCaig poems

Queen of Scots

Red hair uncombed
breakfast untouched
royal foot kicks the adoring Spaniel

John Brown & Queen Victoria

John smoothes his kilt
dreaming of Buckingham Palace
no midgie picnics.

Cathy Scott

Haiku

Poor widow.
He had been kind but lazy
few hens, leaking hoose,
worry

Lesley McLeod

The slimy path heaved with small frogs and mudskippers emerging
from the swamp. Droplets of rain falling from the overhanging leaves
answered the sound of their plopping.

Haiku - The Bookcase

A book, a ship
waiting to transport me
to a different shore.

Freda Bayne

Haiku

(from *Baiting the Fish* by Kathleen Jamie)

Icy mist
fish
frozen? No, asleep
watch him leap
a slap in the face

John Edmondson

M y senses taken in
I grasp your promise.
N o rancour on my breath
T he day you stop my heart.

Haiku 1

A short climb.
Thirty-one Munros
seen in the moment
before the rain.

Haiku 2

The old man
exhaled his last
parcelled up
in jolly striped pyjamas.

Part three

LOUISE FLOWER Christil Trumpet 2007

Andrew Philip

Dream Family Holiday

We were together, the four of us:
the bay had its arms around us
and the sea whispered towards us;
the sun grinned over us,
gulls and gannets laughed with us
and the sand sighed at us.
Then I woke up: one of us
still slept, one was gone from us
and one had not yet come to us.

An Event Peculiar tae this Pairt o the Planet

That nicht, the nation we'd aye been
deed an waukent in a new airt:

the Stane o Destiny licht as ony pillae,
saft an warm as a fresh floury bap;
touns and clachans soomin
wi the souch o steel drums
gettin made fae auld shortbreid tins;
the actual angels aw aroun
tummlin their wulkies i' the air;

an naebody hinkin ocht o peyin for it
as the unkent heroes o this new age
gaed for their messages
or a nip an a hauf like the day afore

but smilin tae theirsels
quaitlike i' the open streets.

Renewables

Sleek white singers of the skyline—
hither and yon

you appear
crowded in chorus and lauding

the wind for its pressure and speed.
So few hear

your voices
even filtering through the grid:

how can we tell if your rank and file
will prevail against

the breakers
massed at our littoral fears?

Ron Ferguson

Did I ever tell you how beautiful Orkney is?

The summer light in Orkney is translucent, ethereal. At 11pm it is still brightish. I love these long evenings when the wind drops, and everything goes still. The waves are lapping gently against the boats. At times like this Orkney seems like the Garden of Eden.

That was how one of Orkney's favourite sons, Edwin Muir, saw it in certain moods. As he looked from his native island of Wyre, he reflected:

One foot in Eden still, I stand
And look across the other land.

It's easy to see why artists have flocked to this northern archipelago. They have tried to capture the changing light in their landscapes and seascapes. Dr Stanley Cursiter, a Kirkwall lad who became the Queen's Painter and Limner in Scotland, is only one of many who have been entranced by the quality of the light.

In the summer evenings, the Viking St Magnus Cathedral stands bathed in sunshine, its red and yellow sandstone soft and welcoming. The Cathedral is itself a festival in stone. The spectacular contemporary stained glass window at the west end of the nave, unveiled in 1987 to mark the 850th anniversary of the founding of the Cathedral, has light as its theme. The window uses various ancient and modern Orkney motifs - Maeshowe, a fish, the Ring of Brodgar, the Flotta flare, and the omnipresent corn. In the mornings, the blue glass dominates, but the afternoon sun sets fire to the central golden circle and showers radiance into the nave.

Orkney weddings are normally held on summer evenings. The soft sunlight, streaming through the kaleidoscopic prism of the west window, magically transfigures strong Orcadian farming brides into mysterious Nordic princesses.

This is the season of visitors. The city and royal burgh of Kirkwall is thronging with people from all over the world. There is a veritable Babel of tongues - Norwegian, French, German, American, Japanese.

On a day like today, people become smitten with the islands. Many proclaim a determination to return to live - and a few do, fleeing the busy south, crossing the Pentland Firth accompanied by a goat, looking for the simple life.

Ah, but if only it were so simple. The shadow, as always, crosses the Garden of Eden. As the season changes, darkness and light intermingle, like wheat and tares. Edwin Muir again:

> *The world's great day is growing late,*
> *Yet strange these fields that we have planted*
> *So long with crops of love and hate.*
> *Time's handiworks by time are haunted,*
> *And nothing now can separate*
> *The corn and tares compactly grown.*

Towards winter, after a fleeting autumn. The days become shorter. The winds howl. Some people suffer from S.A.D. - Seasonally Affective Disorder - a depression caused by lack of light. The summer optimism has evaporated.

Living on an Orkney croft in January is not a simple life. This is when the visitor with the goat heads back, older and wiser, to the bright lights and the busy city. Urban life seems not so bad.

The reality is that an island is the worst place to escape to: islands are by definition insular, and there is no escape. You still have to face yourself, and the self you face in North Ronaldsay is the same self you despaired over in London or Glasgow. There is no return to innocence, to the Garden of Eden. There is no way back.

> *The armorial weed in stillness bound*
> *About the stalk; these are our own.*
> *Evil and good stand thick around*
> *In the fields of charity and sin*
> *Where we shall lead our harvest in.*

Yet the darkness produces great art, too. Out of depression and blackness, out of the shadow self, out of a sense even of the absence of God, great music and poetry and drama, deep in the soul, spring. The artist reaches for the darker colours of the palette. Duncan McLean sits in Stenness, watching the words of his next novel on a screen before him. Peter Maxwell Davies walks around his cottage in Sanday, close to turbulent seas, then writes down turbulent notes.

> *Yet still from Eden springs the root*
> *As clean as on the starting day.*

Time takes the foliage and the fruit
And burns the archetypal leaf
to shapes of terror and of grief
Scattered along the winter way.

Then slowly, Spring. There are days when the gales may reach 120mph, and you know you are in a wind, not the wee breezes that southerners complain about. It was said of the town of Moose Jaw in Saskatchewan that one day the wind stopped and all the inhabitants fell down. For Moose Jaw, read Kirkwall.

St Magnus Cathedral now stands as a great defiant rock, a shelter in the storm.

I love the turbulence and the passion of the seas, the conflict, the clashes of colours, then the peace after the storm. No. Forget passive Eden. Keep the illusory simple life. Welcome complexity, subtlety, grace.

What had Eden ever to say
Of hope and faith and pity and love
Until was buried all its day
And memory found its treasure trove?
Strange blessings never in Paradise
Fall from these beclouded skies.

'Live in Orkney,' wrote Eric Linklater, 'and you know the meaning of summer, the meaning of winter. The year is a living thing, and you live with it. As the months lighten, you pass from the extravagant roughness of a limitless ocean to - on occasional days - the idyllic beauty of life in the midst of a sleeping sea. You are intimately concerned with nature and the procreant forces of the earth. You may have been heroic under the pressure of winter; you will now be happy in the benison of summer.'

Yes, the summer again. This is a benediction of a day - enjoy it while it is here. Did I ever tell you how beautiful Orkney is in the summer? How exquisite the light is?

Our Lady of Yesnaby

Nearing the end of the journey,
at the edge of the cliff.

The figure beckons me from the mist,
leading me on.
A smile plays on her lips,
but her eyes are hollow, as if
she has wept herself out.
She has seen things which a safe eye
should not behold.
She has seen into things
which cannot be endured.

Her cloak is a translucent blue,
but is ripped in places.
Come, she says,
for I have knowledge to impart.
I have gifts for your journey.
She is too mysterious for me -
yet too alluring to walk away from.
She lives on the edge
of danger.
The waves clash down below
with a mesmeric rhythm.

She beckons to me again,
Our Lady of Sorrows and Danger.

Nigel Wheale

The soul stands open

'I'd give you my heart,' says the difficult man,
    whose glance is just my father.

'Do you bide here? Where do I bide?'
    asks the lady locked in to her self.

'Is it more difficult to draw a skyline
    or a horse's tail?' demands the mind-racing man.

He's given me a new title,' says the proud wyf,
    'I'm the erse-wiper noo.'

'Your face is so long you'll fall over it,'
    says the sharp one.

'Puss, Puss!' These lives so refined
    they don't even spend a name on the cat.

'I've never taken the big boat,' she admits,
    nine decades on this island that has been enough.

'But I don't think she saw the mystery,'
    says our lady of language salad.

'What do you want?' I say, too shortly.
    'I want - such a lot. I want one of you
    to take me - where I'm going to play.'

'And how's the affair going?' asks the devout lady,
    brightly. Then, 'Watch yourself round some of these old wyves,
    they can be right tartars.'

I'm irritably checking date stamps in his fridge.
   'This cheese has turned to stone,' I tell him.
   He replies, 'Aye, that's older than God's dog.'

'I saw you and your feet were alight,' said Mother,
   'Oh strike me into unconsciousness.'

And now, whatever life is, has quit the body
it no longer needs, and leaves a small, cold child
curled about nothing. Let's not be sad in this world.

Dear John,

Light is breaking like a heart over Hoy
and the islands are feline tonight,
grey velvet flexing under the cloudscape.
The bleached trace of fence posts
and power lines quarter the land,
and the fields are shaved like landing strips
in the raw truth of extraction.
None of our feuding painter friends catch this, John,
can I say, they all dress it up, this island,
for who would show its rawness and cruelties?
You painted the bay and Flow for me,
insisting that you leave out the power lines,
and the waymarking buoy, which you regretted.
Then your last painting, the burning vision
that caught every eye in the Back Room Gallery -
unreal, holy Hoy dressed in azure and gold,
surely more the alpine summits
under which you lived your other, exiled life
amid the cold strangeness of Switzerland.
Net lines curve across the drawing tide
as the fish and seal weave desperately to cheat them.

Now a distant land briefly knuckles at the skyline, then vanishes,
that other world of force-multipliers and sodium skies
from which we all mistakenly feel reprieved.
The shoreline rocks are full of waiting.
The Flow tenses around the wake of a single vessel,
and the numberless dead of the sea fix her with their empty gaze,
here, where seas have bled upon skerries.
The island children are playing out in this high cold evening.
They quad-bike furiously over the perfect brae,
and how you would love to hear them, John.
A hare lies smoothed by the cool flows of air,
pale fur rings each eye, her pelt blonde-tipped.
But now the light is gone, the bay blank-faced,
the braes and feas mute, and our Virgil wakes to sing
the chastely rising star world, the asterisms we too gazed upon.
'Indigo night, my silent friend', you'd written
in that other life, those other lives, we've all undergone.
Does an unknown hand still settle upon your hand, John,
does your Guide still brush your cheek with a wing?
Are you still catching the Devil by the tail, John?
He surely hasn't caught you, in those blessed calm fields,
azure and gold, where you said we shall meet again,
you wrote to us all, in your perfect manner.
And I'm just as sure we won't, except for this dear recalling,
seeing you in the mantle of light, John,
around the feas of Hoy at evening.

Margaret Storr

Pre-nuptial

Nellie Wilkinson peeped into the dining room. Nobody there; it was safe to take another look at the wedding gifts arranged on the sideboard. She felt the need for reassurance, and hoped that the sight of the domestic goods displayed there would make tomorrow's wedding seem less intimidating. John was a kind and gentle man – but had Papa himself been like that before he had finally won Mama's hand? Could her beloved mother have willingly abandoned the security and comfort of her family to set up her own home with such a man as Papa?

Or, too dreadful to contemplate, had Mama needed to escape, as Nellie now did? Nellie had never known her grandfather Dennis. Had he been...? Fear and filial duty blocked Nellie's mind from going further. Mama had warned her, just this morning, that God had ordained a wife should obey her husband in all things, as children should obey their parents and as the Church, the Bride of Christ, obeyed her Lord.

Nellie ran a shaking finger around the gilded rim of a fluted teacup. Next week the set would be in her own home, in her own little sideboard, waiting for her, no, for *them*, when the honeymoon in Scarborough was over.

A separate, recurrent anxiety arose in Nellie's mind – what actually *happened* on a honeymoon? Mama had said mysteriously that it was all because Eve had stolen the apple, that women ever since had suffered the fruits of her original disobedience, and that it was for Nellie's husband to teach her all she needed to know.

The noisy clatter of boots on polished wood interrupted Nellie's thoughts. Her youngest brother – it could only be Abson – had neglected again to change into his slippers and there would be scuffmarks on the wooden surrounds, mud on the Turkey carpet and trouble for the lad.

'Abson!' she warned, and then gasped as he punched out the seat of the nearest dining chair, leaving a gaping trapezoid hole in the frame.

'*Abson!*'

The boy grinned cheerfully, dropped the leather-covered wooden shape on the floor and moved on to the next chair.

'Abson, what are you *doing?*'

In reply, her brother pointed skywards, rolled his eyes piously and said, 'Message from the Lord above!'

'Ab-*son!*'

Her voice was sharp. Naughtiness was one thing and could be (and was) forgiven in a boy, but blasphemy was another matter altogether. Today Papa's sharp ears were not safely far away in his office.

Abson took no notice of his sister but proceeded to punch out a further seven seats. He picked up six from the floor and thrust the pile at his sister.

'Front parlour!' he commanded. 'And don't ask questions!'

He tucked the three remaining disembodied seats under an arm and opened the door for his burdened sister, sweeping an exaggerated bow and waving her through into the hall.

When they reached the parlour, he kicked aside the Persian rugs and laid three of the wooden shapes in a row in the middle of the room, then five behind these. In front of the newly-created rows stood a padded footstool on which sat a red velvet cushion decorated with gold tassels. Beside it, Abson gently laid down the last wooden seat.

'Why? What's this all about?' Nellie wanted to know, but Abson merely turned down the corners of his mouth, shrugged his shoulders and began to push the reproduction Sheraton chairs back against the walls of the parlour. It was fine, elegant furniture, saved from the disaster seven years earlier when Papa had been deceived by Mama's brother into making an unwise investment. Uncle Reginald had not been invited to tomorrow's wedding.

There was the sound of approaching footsteps – many of them – and into the parlour came a procession headed by Mr Wilkinson. Following him were his wife, two of his sons and three of his daughters. The elderly housekeeper, the parlourmaid and the tweeny brought up the rear.

'John!' the stentorian voice boomed. 'You will take your place, front right, behind the kneelers. George! Beside your brother. Abson! Beside George.'

Kneelers? Why? Am I to be married here, today? But there's no vicar. Oh Heavens! Has Papa cancelled the wedding? Are we to give thanks for my release from a marriage Papa thinks is beneath me?

As the boys moved to their appointed places, Wilkinson turned to his daughters.

'Ellen, you will take the *second* kneeler behind your brothers. Next, Edith. Mary! Release Lucy's hand! She must learn to stand on her own feet. Mrs Oldroyd, shut the door. You and the others, behind my children.'

As the girls and the servants took their places, Nellie glanced at her mother, who was now standing behind the single wooden seat, and facing her household. To her dismay, Nellie noticed tears trickling down her mother's cheeks, and anger rose and stuck in the girl's throat.

Whatever might be planned, Nellie knew that the empty place beside her was for the eldest daughter, Annie, dead two years now, but always present, a place laid for her at table, a space reserved for her in the family pew. When Annie had fallen ill, proper medical treatment had been deemed too costly. Nellie's fingers clenched over the scar on her right palm.

'Your sister has gone to a better place!' Swish! The cane had come down. 'Do you selfishly grieve at her new-found joy?' Swish! 'Do you dare to question God's purpose?' Swish. Crack! The ferrule of the cane had become embedded in Nellie's hand.

Please, please, Mama, don't let him see you weeping.

'Aaow!'

'George!' His father's voice boded ill for the boy.

'But he dug me in the ribs, father!'

'Ah, *Abson!* You will see me afterwards.'

Nellie noted with relief, approval and dread for Abson, that the boy's diversionary tactics had given their mother the chance to wipe away her tears unobserved.

Tomorrow cannot come a moment too soon. If you cancel my wedding, Papa, I shall elope.

Wilkinson took his place behind the padded footstool. He inflated his chest and drew himself up to his full height. He was a tall, well-built man, broad-shouldered, secure in the knowledge of his own superiority. His features were handsome, his eyes dark, and both his hair and full naval set black and curly. No amount of Macassar oil could subdue the aggressive wiriness of his hair and beard.

'We,' he said and paused, fixing each with a stern look. 'Are gathered together here.' There was another pause. 'In the sight of God!' His voice rose on the last word.

What is happening? Nellie was trembling.

'Humbly to beseech our Maker to answer our prayers.'

Wilkinson looked at the gathered company; he had their full attention. From the pocket in which he kept his gold turnip watch he extracted a slip of paper. Nellie held her breath. A note from John, saying he could not go through with the wedding?

'The *Methodists*,' Wilkinson sneered, 'a sect which I *despise*.'

The last word this time was delivered in such ringing tones that Nellie half-expected the gas lamps to shatter in their sconces.

'Have,' her father continued, 'published a grave message to their misguided flock in this morning's newspaper. This extract was cut out and delivered to me by one of my clerks, doubtless in the hopes of advancement.'

Wilkinson waved the flimsy piece of newsprint back and forth.

'I shall read it to you, and then we shall all kneel in prayer.'

Weak with relief that John had not jilted her, and wondering what the scandalous Methodist message might be, at the back of her mind Nellie registered that the servants would be kneeling on bare boards. Would Mrs Oldroyd manage to get down that far?

Wilkinson cleared his throat.

'*The social evening*,' he read out, '*arranged for tomorrow.*' There was a dramatic pause. '*Is postponed due to the critical condition of our Queen.*'

Wilkinson looked up at the shocked faces before him.

'You will notice that these supposed men of God cannot even write our Queen's language with grammatical accuracy. Well now, our little schoolmarm, wherein lies their error? Come on, come on. What? Silence? It seems just as well that you have resigned your post.'

Nellie cleared her throat and answered nervously.

'It should read *owing* to the critical condition of our Queen, Father.'

'Yes, well.'

Wilkinson seemed a little disappointed, but rallied and smiled unctuously at his daughter.

'You understand, my *dear* Ellen, what that means?'

What? That I am forgiven for knowing my grammar? That the Methodists might not after all be consigned to everlasting Hell for breaking from the Established Church?

Wilkinson's rictus split further.

'When our gracious Queen dies, there will be no weddings throughout the length and breadth of our land for the period of national mourning. Now,' he paused to check the expression on his daughter's face. 'Let. Us. *Pray!*'

'Oh Lord of Hosts, if it be Thy will, *swiftly* end the suffering of our Gracious Sovereign Lady, Queen Victoria, and take her into Thy loving bosom to rest now in eternal peace. Amen.'

There was a shocked silence.

'Amen,' Wilkinson repeated warningly.

'Amen,' came the ragged chorus.

As Nellie opened her eyes, she saw that her father's were shut, but his smile was even wider.

Diana Hendry

Pollarded Poplars
(for Lars Abrahamson)

Look at the faces they pull
these two old Lears lopped
of their robes and kingly trappings
and shamed into cloaking their poor
bald pates with silly green night caps.

How they growl, snarl and ache
for the lost dominion of youth,
makes fists of their stumps.
Scars, warts and whiskers
are their only regalia who once

had divine rights over the garden
and could stretch a royal limb
in kingly blessing on sparrow
or daisy. Now here comes Lars
with his pad and charcoal to restore

them to grandeur in art's odd kingdom.

Till Diana

Lan Abrahamson
Grez 10maj 07

POPLARS Lars Abrahamson 2007

Hamish Whyte

Saturday night blues at the Chevillon
(for Antti Jaakola)

In the half-lit dining-room
rolling the keys
Antti lingers on the chords
of what we begin to recognise
as one of the classics
but he has to push it on
he's not solo
there's a beat, slow, but a beat
from Hamish at the batterie de cuisine:
brushes on a biscuit tin snare,
assorted pots, pans, bowls, lids -

the piano's out of tune
the drums are pickup
but the quiet voice
with its Baltic edge is true
pulling us all - Swedes, Finns, Scots -
into that Delta philosophy
into the absolute certainty
you can go to church on Sunday
and get drunk all day Monday -

it's nobody's business if you do.

Yesnaby

there's no yes- no- maybe
about Yesnaby
you could write a tune
called 'Yesnaby Cliffs'
and play it on a hardanger fiddle
your fingers would fly to their places
your bow would be a bow
splitting and splicing the sea

Paul Maxton

Fresh Clean Sheets

It's two in the morning and Frank Gibson is doing his laundry when Sasha appears at his door.

'I saw your lights on,' she says.

'This is the thirteenth floor.'

'I needed to see you.' She edges past with a deft smile, shows herself into the tidy living room. She's wearing a long black skirt, white shirt and black bow-tie under a mock croc coat. 'Some leftovers from work,' she says, passing him a soiled polythene poke, her coat creaking. Setting down her Aztec duffle bag, she then says, 'I could murder a drink'.

'What's it to be?'

'Martini and lemonade.'

'You finished the martini last time.'

'You didn't buy anymore?'

He scratches the stubble on his chin while raising his eyes.

'Don't look so serious. What else you got?'

He turns towards the kitchen.

'Any gin?'

'We wiped that out as well.'

'What's left?'

'Smirnoff… Vladivar…?'

'You know I hate Vodka.' She pinches her nostrils and bats her hair. 'Can't stand the smell.'

'Morgan's Spiced?'

She shakes her head. 'Any whisky?'

'We demolished it last week.'

'Bacardi?'

'Maybe; I'll check.'

'With coke?'

His rocks his head. Then: 'I think we can do that.'

'Oh…and bring some forks and plates.'

He pauses at the door, watches her shake smir from her long, sandy hair. He raises his chin, squeezes his Adam's apple. He waits; but she doesn't look his way.

When he returns, she's removed her boots and is stretched out at the foot of the settee, rippling her stockinged toes by the gas fire. Her shirt is open at the neck; the bow-tie framing his mug of vodka on the coffee table.

'Here you go,' he says, carefully laying down the tray with the drink and forks and plates.

'Cheers!' She takes a large swallow of Bacardi, shivers with her eyes closed, then splutters and coughs, grasping her throat.

'Easy,' he says.

She blinks, then gulps another large mouthful. 'Shit, I needed that!' she then says with a shivering smile.

He begins to divvy up the food, forking out the rice, prawns and sweet and sour sauce onto two plates. He empties a poke of prawn crackers into an old casserole dish.

'Any Soy sauce?' she says.

'I'll go see.'

'Oyster sauce would be perfect.'

'I don't know about that.'

He finds Dark and Light in the cupboard in the kitchen, brings both through.

She holds up her empty glass. 'I could kill another.'

He twists his lips, smoothes his hands down his jeans. He looks at her, keeps looking, then nods. 'I'll bring the bottle.'

When he returns with the Bacardi, she is scoffing the food like she hasn't eaten in days. He tops up her glass, pouring a generous measure, then adds some Coke from a can. She dollops the Dark over her food, forks some rice. He watches her eat, jaw working furiously, pausing only to sip her Bacardi.

Her need begins to please him. 'Busy tonight?' he says.

She finishes chewing, hunches her shoulders. 'It was shit,' she then says, staring absently. 'Fucking awful, in fact. It was so quiet I washed the plastic menus...' She swipes her mouth with the back of a hand. '...Then a bunch of drunken bastards came piling in as we were about to close.'

She shakes her head, begins scooping rice into her mouth, the plate raised beneath her chin. Flagging a hand, she then says, 'Fetch me some water. I've a real thirst tonight.'

Her plate is near empty when he returns with the glass. She dunks some prawn crackers into the remains of the sweet and sour, a hand holding back her hair. She then washes the crackers down with the water, gulping it back until she's drained the glass. 'I left my onions,' she says, wiping her hands on her skirt. 'I quit sucking my thumb after I sliced it open peeling onions - I hate onions.' She inspects her thumb, then opens the palm of her hand, begins tracing a finger over the lifelines.

He looks at the stodge on his plate, then sizes up the bottle of vodka. When he hears the washing machine cycle end, he raises his eyes, touches her shoulder on the way to switch on the dryer.

When he returns from the kitchen, she has lit one of his Marlboros. She leans back with a quizzical smile, takes a luxuriant draw, then exhales slowly through her nose, funnelling the smoke 'Thanks,' she says. 'A waitress likes being waited on.'

She looks worn-out; but always does. She told him once that she never uses eye shadow because of the natural darkness around her eyes. The crow's feet she's going to have surgically removed; it's on her list of improvements after having her breasts enlarged, her lips thickened.

She drags her Aztec duffle bag towards her. 'I'm seeing a client tonight.'

'You're welcome to change here.'

'It's not just that.'

He takes a Marlboro from the packet on the table, lights up. Under the lamp light, he can make out the powder on her cheek, the faint wisp of fair hair above her lip. She rubs an eye, then flicks beneath it. 'He'll be here in half an hour. It's just this once - promise.'

'You're kidding?'

'I got kicked out of my place.'

'Why?'

'It's a long story.'

'Try me.'

'Let's just say it wasn't meant to be.'

'Is that it?'

She crawls over to him, rubs her head between his legs. 'Please don't give me a hard time. I need you to understand.' She looks up, eyes wide, expectant.

He takes a puff, exhales; another quick puff, exhales; and another, exhales. 'Shit,' he then says, dunting his forehead with the heel of a hand. 'I don't fucking believe you.'

'Don't get like that,' she says. 'You look mean when you get intense.'

He breaks her grip around his shins and moves to the window. Leaning both hands on the sill, he lowers his head, then looks up, taking in the sprawl of tiny bright lights with the dark ribbon of the Clyde sandwiched between; the airport lights further off, blue and blinking.

'I can stay with you afterwards,' she says. 'Would you like that?'

He glances to his right; takes in the arc of lights over the Erskine Bridge. She comes up behind him, massages his neck. And it feels good; her touch.

'You know I like you,' she says. 'I feel safe with you.' She turns him towards her, taking his head in both hands. 'Tell me there's no bad energy.'

'There's no bad energy.'

'It's important.'

He nods. 'I'm good.'

She studies his face, twists her lips. 'I can't find your aura,' she says. 'You've normally a strong aura.'

'I don't know about that shit.'

'You're mad with me.'

He squeezes his nose. 'No.'

'You're a crap liar.'

'I'm fine. Everything's fine.' He shrugs. 'I'm always fine.'

'Got skinned at the bookies?'

'No.'

'Your back giving you jip?'

He raises his head and laughs.

'Whatever...' She rummages through her bag, then holds up a hair brush. 'Do you mind?'

He takes over the brush, begins working her hair the way she has shown him; long deliberate strokes, fanning it out at the end. Her hair is important; never dyed, washed every second day. He prefers when it's plaited; thinks she looks Scandinavian.

'I phoned my psychic today,' she says, picking at some split ends.

He pauses to sip his vodka, holding it back before swallowing. He then lights another Marlboro, takes a deep draw, his head nodding steadily.

'Okay, I know it doesn't grab you…' She shrugs.

'Go on,' he says, passing her the cigarette. 'What did they cook up this time?'

She exhales, flicking ash from her skirt. 'You're in a shit mood.'

He pulls against a tug of hair.

'Ahh, careful!' she says.

'Sorry.'

'My lover killed me in a previous life,' she then says. 'What do you make of that?'

She sounds genuinely proud, as if she's achieved something.

'You *paid* to hear that?'

'Some of us are more spiritual than others.' She checks her watch. 'Shit, I'll need to get changed. You can watch. I know you like to watch.'

'I don't know,' he says.

'Don't be like that. Stay. There's time.'

He hands her back the brush, watches her dump the mess of the Aztec bag on the settee. He sits opposite, watching.

'I forgot the book I said I'd bring,' she says.

'How to improve your life?'

'Goal setting,' she says. Then: 'It's important to know what you want.'

'Like you?'

'Sure. I don't want to be a waitress in a pissy restaurant - or doing *this* for the rest of my life.' She fixes the last catch to her stockings, then holds her legs out, paddling them like she's sitting at the edge of a swimming pool. 'It's a means to an end.' She looks at herself in a compact. 'Take you,' she says, puckering her lips, applying lipstick. 'In the short term you need a job - anything; long term you should consider training, going to college. But you need to set a time frame.' She opens and closes her eyes, pouts at the mirror.

'You've got it all sussed.'

She lights a Marlboro, cocks her head. 'So, Frankie boy; what do you want to do? Who do you want to be?'

'The hell do I know.'

'You must have some idea?'

He shrugs, curls his thumbs around the waist band of his jeans. 'A cowboy? I've always wanted to be a cowboy.'

'You're a cowboy alright.'

He raises his mug to her. 'Okay,' he then says. 'Australia – I've always fancied my luck out there.'

'They don't let in ex-cons.'

'Well that's *that* scuppered!'

'Focus on what you're good at.'

'Drinking – I was so good the Lusset fired me.' He holds his mug up and smiles. 'Too busy sampling the product!'

'Sounds like you've some thinking to do.'

'I'm good at thinking.'

'You can do too much thinking.' She arches an eyebrow as she slowly exhales. 'Why not try a business course - like me?'

He pours another neat Vodka, throws it back in one. He likes the warmth, the instant fire in his belly, the way it then rises up his throat to his ears.

'We could do it together,' she says. 'Be a team. You're always saying we should get together.'

'Serious?'

'Sure.'

'No; *really*?'

'Why not?'

He raises his eyebrows, purses his lips. 'I'd need to think it through.' Then: 'This isn't one of your schemes?'

'*Schemes?*'

'You never see anything through. Something always… *happens.*'

'Fuck you!'

'Always the lady.'

She takes a sharp draw on her cigarette, exhales slowly. Then: 'I'm trying to help.'

'I don't need help.'

'It could be a fresh start.' She shrugs, looks away.

'For *us*?'

She smiles; then stands up, does a twirl. 'What do you think? Do I turn you on?'

'You look good. Real good.'

'But do I turn you on?'

The basque is tight and stretched; her buttocks dimpled; and blue veins are showing on the backs of her thighs; but hey, he thinks, she's alright - not bad for thirty seven. He smacks her backside.

'Steady!'

He watches the imprint of his hand slowly fade.

'Soon have enough for the boob job,' she then says.

'Your tits are fine. I like your tits.'

'They're too small,' she says, squeezing her breasts together.

'Your lips are fine, too.'

'You like my lips?'

'They're hot.'

'You don't need to say that.'

'You said you wanted more honesty.'

'Did I?' She frowns. Then: 'Why are you looking at me like that? Am I getting in your hair?'

He runs his hand over his bald head, grins.

'Look, Frank. You're a good man; a decent man - but I can't love you. I can't love anyone.' She sips her Bacardi, then shakes her head.

'You did in your previous life - give or take a murder.'

'You should set your sights higher.'

'Like having Oyster sauce in the cupboard?'

'I'm serious.'

'I'm a loser, Sash. That's why I can't hold a job.'

She checks her watch. 'Is the bedroom okay?'

'I think so.'

'Mind if I check?'

'On you go.'

He follows her into the bedroom, watching the exaggerated swing of her buttocks.

'I told you to shift the mirror,' she says, frowning.

'I don't remember.'

'It's still opposite the bed.'

'Is that bad?'

'It drains you of energy while you sleep.'

'Sounds bad.'

She grasps the nape of her neck, works her muscles, grimacing. 'Can I borrow some aftershave?' she says.

'Sure.'

When he returns from the bathroom, she has arranged some crystals on the coffee table. He passes her the aftershave.

'Wish me luck,' she says.

'You'll be fine.'

She turns the bottle upside down in her palm, then touches her throat, cheeks and wrists. 'You'd better split.'

He glances at the starburst clock over the mantelpiece and nods.

'Give me half an hour,' she says.

'I'll be back,' he says.

'I'll be waiting,' she says.

'The tumble dryer is set,' he says. 'We can have fresh clean sheets.'

He takes the stairs down the high-rise, cuts across the road with all the bed-sits, then through the new housing scheme with its iron arches and play area. He sits on a swing and swigs from the neck of a Smirnoff bottle. He likes the sound the cap makes when he twists it open and closed. He likes the silence and the darkness and the shadows. He likes the way the clouds stand out in front of the three-quarter moon. He likes not having to get up in the morning and no longer having a wife. He likes the fog of his breath in the still, evening air. When he's finished the bottle, he tosses it into some bushes; but it doesn't smash. Curling his arms around the chains, he lets his head fall to his chest, his feet peddling the tarmac, lurching to and fro. He gives Sasha the benefit of an extra ten minutes before heading back. It's four in the morning, the beginning of November with nobody else around. He likes being drunk enough to care and then not to care; drunk enough to understand everything and nothing at the same time. He uses the stairwell, pausing at the top of each flight to catch his breath. A fucking cowboy, he says to himself on the twelfth landing. He laughs and shakes his head. Sifting through a matchbox, he is unable to find a match that isn't spent, but keeps the cigarette in his mouth anyway. He lets himself into the flat and picks through the living room, looking for anything different, foreign. He pauses at the coffee table, picks up the bow-tie and clasps it firmly in his hand. He chaps his bedroom door but there's only a faint sobbing. He pauses, then turns the handle and lets the door swing slowly open.

'Don't turn on the light!'

The moonlight throws a crucifix over the bed. Sasha is under the covers, whimpering. 'What the fuck's happened?'

She snivels loudly. 'Please, don't come near me, please!'

He lies down beside her, pauses before reaching out.

'Don't touch me!' she snarls.

He lightly brushes back some hair from her face.

'Please don't touch me!'

A slash runs diagonally from the tip of her ear to her lips. He grips the bow-tie tighter in his other hand, understanding that the dampness under his head is blood. 'It's okay,' he says. 'Frankie's here,' he says. 'You don't need to worry about anything,' he says. 'Frankie's going to take care of you.'

'No!' she screams. 'No!'

His chest rises with the excitement of the tumble dryer nearing the end of its cycle.

Cheers

On news of my bother's death,
I looked at his painting a lot.
The painting has nine panels;
each with a scene with chairs.
Simple, elongated chairs
with a single spar for the high back.
But in each scene,
the chairs have a suggestion of movement:
the legs aren't straight, front or rear,
and the backs have subtle curves.
Then the deer started to appear.
Like a revelation.
The seat became the body;
the top, above the spar, their ears.
I began looking at my own chairs
in a different light.
They grazed at the kitchen table
and shied in my presence.
Returning from his funeral,
on the A9
between Drumochter and the Slochd Summit,
there were chairs everywhere.
I'd never seen so many before.
They were feeding on the ridges near the road
and roaming the hills further away.
Nearing Brora,
a deer sprung out
and I stood on the brake.
It was a buck;
a fawn.
And he turned to speak,
perfect in the headlights,
before loping into the darkness.

Clare Gee

A poem not about 'it'

I thought I wanted to write about 'it'
but I don't.

I thought I needed to write about 'it'
but I couldn't.

I tried to write about 'it'
but it wouldn't come
and I can't.

I thought it would help
come to terms
take stock
exorcise the demons
let me move on
deal with 'it'
but I just want to forget 'it'.

Learn from 'it' – yes
feel safe again – yes
but write about 'it'

No.

Pottering in Pyjamas

'I pottered in my pyjamas all day' she said
relishing the memory of luxuriant laziness.

She'd got a lot done, house and garden
the treat of not having to get dressed
making every success and task achieved
doubly satisfying.

When I was little I once went to bed with my best dress on
peacocks and a white lace collar
the logic being it would save time
getting ready for school.

I got bollocked for it.

Highway Maintenance

For weeks they were there
tied awkwardly on top of each other
ribbons blowing - getting grubby
cellophane wrapping - flapping in tatters.

I drive past every day
(except Saturdays and Sundays)
where the road bends up the hill to the left
as the lamp posts run out.

I look each time
not knowing what happened there
I guess - go cold
drive on up the hill.

A few days ago - I'm not sure which
as I drove past
a van - highway maintenance
a man - fluorescent patched donkey jacket
meticulously placing the dead flowers
in a line on the verge.

Must be a distraction.

You can just make them out
if you know where to look.

They blend in with the rubbish.

Gordon Marriott

Doorway to the Past (extract from a novel in progress)

'So, where's the Tardis ?' quipped Dougie Rimmer, science correspondent for the *The Daily Express* to his fellow hack Tim O'Leary of *The Irish Times* as they entered the Embassy Suite of the Strand Hotel. The press release hadn't really inspired either of them to attend a demonstration of 'time travel' but it was the silly season so they were grateful for anything coming their way which even remotely gave an opportunity for an individual angle.

'Looks like the bar's not open either,' Tim moaned, surveying the grilled shutters; the only evidence of hospitality being jugs of iced water placed at strategic intervals around a horse-shoe table arrangement encircling a medical examination couch, with a chair placed at either end of it. A third chair was in the centre of the couch next to a small table on which there was a lamp and notepad.

So, up to now, nothing even remotely resembling Dr Who's time travel machine.

Settling themselves, Dougie glanced around recognizing a few other people from the nationals, together with the usual bunch of local reporters; and typical for an event such as this, a sprinkling of freelancers and staff reporters from esoteric magazines such as *Prediction* and *Kindred Spirit*. One identified the latter immediately from their attire – the women in floating kaftans or long flowing skirts; the men mainly bearded, and/or with pony-tail hairstyles.

Rimmer sensed it was going to be a long and tedious morning. The journalist from *Outlook*, Stella Atkinson, sitting next to him, appeared to be of the same opinion as the double doors at the far end of the suite opened, and a small procession of five people began to walk slowly towards them to the strains of floaty New Age music. 'Oh Christ, no' she muttered to herself rather than to anyone in particular, and scribbled something on her pad.

Dougie leaned in towards Stella's bent head whispering 'I think I can take about an hour of this at the most, Stella. Could you put on a faint or something and I'll escort you out of here?' 'Yeah, I used to be able to do quite a convincing faint at the Uni's drama society, but that was a few years ago,' she whispered back, with a smile.

The procession had now reached the couch area. The bespectacled, bald-headed small man who had been leading it stepped towards the assembly. Dressed in his dapper suit and clip bow tie, he reminded Rimmer of his old prep school headmaster. Meanwhile, the other members of the group had taken their places around the couch. Two middle-aged women were seated on each end, and a young man with short-cropped blonde hair on the chair beside the couch. He'd taken up the pad and pen, so it was obvious what his role would be in the proceedings.

The final member of the group was a tall, blue-eyed strikingly attractive woman with shoulder length jet-black hair. Dressed in a high-necked white jumper, contrasting tight black lycra leggings, with bare feet, she remained standing next to the seated scribe as the main lights dimmed. 'Blondie' turned on the table lamp, which cast a pink rosy glow around the scene.

'Ladies and gentlemen of the Press, good morning, and thank you for coming,' the small man began in short, staccato tones in an accent Rimmer couldn't place, but which might have been mid-European. 'I am Doctor Alexander Blondin.' Dougie muttered to Stella 'Oh God, not a tightrope act as well.' As she didn't acknowledge the jibe he assumed she wasn't old enough to have heard of the famous man who'd walked across the Niagara Falls.

'No relation,' said Blondin (allowing himself a small pause). 'It was a pseudonym anyway.' Rimmer frowned. He didn't know that. 'However, we shall be doing a somewhat different type of tightrope walking today,' Blondin went on – 'treading the fine line that exists between' (another pause) 'life – and death'.

If he goes on at this rate we'll all be in our graves before he's finished, Dougie thought, giving Stella another look, which she picked up. He pointed at his watch to the top of the hour, to which she nodded. Dougie pondered what they might do after they'd made their escape. He'd got a thing about redheads. Young Stella was a fine example of that breed, with a body to match. A bit like that one up at the front, but different hair, and shorter too... Keep your mind on the task in hand, Rimmer. What was the old boy on about now?

The introductions continued. Blondin walked over to the statuesque woman who had been the cause of his distraction. 'Last, but by no means least, our time pilot, Miss Danielle Frazer.' The 'time pilot' produced the obligatory smile, whilst remaining tall and erect, her eyes focused on some point at the end of the room.

You can fly me any time, Danielle, Dougie mused, once more taking in her athletic body, trying to making a guess at her age. Perhaps a well-preserved forty? The 'crows' claws' were just about visible under her otherwise flawless eye makeup. More his age group than the carrot-top next door, giving Stella a sideways glance, who was dutifully looking at Blondin. She probably works out, or does Yoga. He noted her firm, musculo quadriceps femorals through the thin Lycra leggings; his biology speciality was making him more appreciative. Get a grip on yourself, Rimmer. But at the same time his imagination was goading him with images of Danielle gripping on him with those awesome thighs…

Walking towards the journalists, Blondin was continuing his monologue: 'The actual origins of the Christos technique seem to be lost in time' - once again managing a half smile. 'Indeed, the name itself is a bit of an enigma, but seems to be credited to a Mrs Parkhurst, whose first husband learned the technique from a Mr Bill Swygard who once lived in the United States, where it is sometimes known as the Swygard procedure. No one, however seems to know where, or from whom, Mr Swygard learned the technique.' Rimmer noted Blondin pronounced his w's as v's, so maybe German? Maybe it is 'Svygard'…or maybe it's just a fake accent.

Rimmer glanced at his watch, muttering to himself. He'd got twenty minutes to wrap this up. They'd been told nothing of what they'd come to hear apart from this rather obscure term; or about the so-called 'technique' – and how it is connected to 'time-travelling'. Time was certainly travelling for him at the moment. Time is both precious and valuable in journalism, as are words, and this fellow was more than over-using them. Rimmer brought his attention back to the speaker.

'Certainly, the main instigator of the technique was Gerald Glaskin, whose two books *Windows of the Mind* and *Worlds Within* were published in the early seventies, but are now out of print.' Blondin droned on, seemingly oblivious of the increasing disquiet of his audience.

'Well, they would be, wouldn't they?' Dougie whispered to Stella, who stifled a giggle, catching the eye of Blondin, who glared at them – a couple of naughty schoolchildren in his class. Rimmer became more sceptical of the man as he wove an intricate web of obscurity around the origins of the process; making a mental note to track down the two book references.

Blondin began walking to their table, his beady little eyes peering through the rimless spectacles, stopping directly in front of Stella.

'Were you thinking of leaving, Ms Atkinson?' - asking the question in an accusing, squeaky tone.

Stella braved it out; the ex-drama student's face moulding itself into desired features to suit her words: 'I was just saying to my colleague here I was feeling a bit queasy... perhaps the room temperature?'... Her voice trailed off.

Blondin, looking at his watch then straight back to her, announced 'Madam, you were going to put on a fake faint in just seven minutes. Could I suggest you leave us *now?* You are obviously not the least bit interested in the demonstration.'

Stella's face went genuinely white. Dougie could feel his turning red. Rising from his chair he glared at the little man. 'Now look here, Mr Blondin' (deliberately omitting his self-imposed title) 'I don't think you have the right to make that sort of a remark. Everyone can see Ms Atkinson is clearly unwell.' There were a number of murmurs of assent. Blondin spun around, his thin face twisted into a sneer. 'As it was *you* who suggested this charade to the lady, Sir, you are hardly in the position of acting as her knight errant.' The focus was now on Dougie, who wondered how the hell he knew that. Maybe the guy had something to offer after all.

Dougie glanced down at Stella, still looking visibly shaken; then gathering his wits replied, 'I think our first priority is to get Ms Atkinson into some fresh air, Mr Blondin.' With general sounds of approval Dougie helped Stella to her feet, heading towards the door.

'Dougie, I'm really feeling very groggy,' her voice now all but a whisper.

Blondin's mocking voice rang behind them before they reached the door. He was obviously looking at his watch again. 'You have just thirty seconds. I don't think you're going to make it.'

Dougie felt Stella growing heavier and heavier. He put his arm around her waist as she clung to his shoulder. Someone supported her on the other side, but after about three more steps she slumped into their arms. As they reached the door he looked back, seeing the mocking smile on Blondin's face.

Behind him; still standing erect as a statue, the cold blue eyes of Danielle were boring into his own, imprinting messages in his mind. Messages he knew he would not, and could not, ignore.

K.K. Scott

Socks

The socks matched
    so
       I
          took
            them

they were alone,
bunched on the floor
'ah ha,' I thought, 'a gift
from the sock deity.'
A sacrifice to neatness,
banality and conservatism
for socks,
whether matched or not
are incongruous to the
tidiness of the living room.

Your socks are fine now,
albeit
a bit odiferous,
stretched out
over my bloody bunions,
flanking the walls of my
crusted corns,
         warming warts.

They are everything a sock
is supposed to be.
Now when do you want them back?

Marriage

was not written on my life list
next to Elf Owl
    below
Arctic Tern
    neither
before nor after
Toucan.

Somehow
    I found myself
        trancelike
repeating the phrase
        'solemnly and seriously'
with my American sibilant S
        in front of a room
full
        of Orcadians dressed in
        party clothes.

Holding the hand of a
    handsome stranger
my new husband.

I felt swollen
    with love, my
stubby fingers
    warm and
        comfortable in
his hand.

Time slowed,
    stopped and was
        suspended in the
dust motes of afternoon sun.

Cold,
northern light
    framed my sister's
hair as a halo might.

Transported
     outside my physical
       self
I felt weightless,
     disembodied energy.
Pure love.

Elizabeth Coward

She slammed the drawer shut and stuffed the remaining clothes into her rucksack. She could hear the battle raging downstairs. Mother bellowing, father swallowing, empty beer bottles multiplying on the kitchen floor. She was sure it was about money again. It was always about money. Her mother's favourite phrase 'yer feckin useless' was on rapid-fire repeat, the guttural tones driving her father further into his bottle.

She hated them both, her mother for being so hard, her father for being so weak. Thank god she was finally leaving this shite-house. Even if Derek didn't get the ticket arrangements sorted in time, she knew she'd still go. Just go to the station and get on a train. If she didn't get out of here soon, she might commit an unspeakable act.

Bump, bump, bump, the rucksack thumped behind her as she dragged it down the stairs. She knew they would hear. At least the yelling stopped.

'Is that you, Bridget? What in Jesus' name is that racket?'

Her mother stepped into the hallway from the kitchen.

'And just where do ya think yer aff to? What you needin' such a big pack fer? Ya think yer goin' somewhere?'

'Ah am goin'' she said to the bottom stair. Please don't let her make a scene, she prayed. She sucked in her breath and held it for a moment.

'Just let me go, Ma, ah'm leavin.'

'Yer what?!'

'You heard me.' She exhaled.

She looked straight into her mother's eyes, expecting an onslaught.

'Oh dear lard in heaven!' Her mother covered her eyes and turned away.

More quietly she asked, 'Are you sure?'

'Yeah,' Bridget replied, 'sort of.'

Her mother turned around. Her eyes were wet.

'You're only nineteen.' The voice was soft and pleading.

'Ah'm twenty!'

'Only twenty?' Louder now, it was almost an insult instead of a fact.

'Ah know what age ah am, mother!'

'There's no need ta get cheeky.' Back again to the soft and low.

She heard the shuffle of her father's footsteps. She could feel his reluctance to get too close without knowing where the bullets were coming from.

She began to move down the steps. Her mother's voice beating at her as she pushed past.

'Ah'm the one who should be gettin' cheeky! It's me that'll suffer! How can you just leave us like this? Without so much as a word! Is this the way to treat us after all we've done fer you?'

Bridget stopped listening. If she didn't she would never go. She opened the front door, heaved her rucksack down the steps and herself after it. Raising it up on her shoulders, she turned to see her mother standing in the doorway. The face told her there was no need for goodbye.

'What do *you* think of all this then?' Her mother barked at her father who was behind her. There was desperation in her voice, a hope that he could somehow keep her there.

'Ah don't know,' he muttered and looked straight at Bridget. She wasn't sure, but she thought she saw him wink.

Galen Brown

Trapped

Old Jack's wife never did cry
when she found her husband gone
but stood by running river
that once, to her, had brought him.

When young Jack had come along
in wooden boat; tent on back
he said he'd come to visit
'Just a night, I'll stay,' he said.

She watched, as he pitched his tent
tall boy with his golden hair
whose strong hands pulled guy lines taut
whose bare back glistened in sun.

That night, to his tent she went
said just a few words; lay down
beside him, sang songs of old.

Fifty years, he stayed.

One Thousand Kilometres Home/ The Emigrant

The air is dry, hot
filled with the sound of
a thousand insects.

Old trainers, dust clogged

pat down on dirt track
so systematic.

I hear engine roar
smell exhaust fumes, soot
with cigarette smoke.

I see white farmer
over-fed, plain white
sun cap, khaki dressed.

I see fence, barbed wire
feel my legs ache, throb
take a chance and run.

Feel legs give way, feel
sweaty hands grab me.

Hear voices, resigned
in southern accent.

They say, 'Go home,
it's not worth it.'

I hear the words
of my woman.

Left caring for
little brother.

'You are worth more
than this,' she said.

Her voice tears at
my mind, my soul.

'Find a new life,'
she said.

Mike Fairbairn

Sunshine and the Tin Chapel

Grant called Sunshine at least seven times and then stopped, remembering the trainer's advice – 'tell them once or they'll just make you say it over and over again, they'll train you!' And that had seemed right for the litter bitten compound where he and Kelly had watched on a forgotten day, with happy faces, as their new dogs circled round them confusedly pleased to be out of the shelter's kennels.

But here – apart now, between broken field edges, Sunshine looked older and the breeze was buffeting through her coat, rushing over her numbed ears. She was not a big dog and had easily run under a low wire fence that marked an end of the land, she wasn't tuned in at all – everything had changed. Through each opening reached, she might come to her friend Cloudy, except she wouldn't. He was hundreds of miles behind – the car god had flung counties, mountain ranges and sea firths between them.

So Grant ran to head her off, spilling his coffee over the rocks and frowning down at his feet that picked at the tussock spoiled land – the land that was his now. At the road, two hundred yards from the building, he stopped and leant forward trying to close his mouth, Sunshine was heading towards him now – cut off at the pass. There he was, he wouldn't do, but there he was. Grant looked all ways up the road – nothing. They were together on an island that was called Orkney, but from where he was standing you'd never know it. Fields and low felt tip moors, houses and farms spotted out across, never closer than a half-mile. But looking, searching for some isle like fact, it was possible to see the dissolving struck match of a lighthouse. From it, inland sheep could calculate that rocky partitions waited for them in the clapping sea.

He dipped a hand under the dog's old collar, and they returned to the Chapel – as he had taken to calling the tin shack of Moorquoy – and around the pocked couchy fields (his fields he again prodded himself) the sky flipped through each index of shade before offering down a soaking curse. They entered through the plywood door and once more Sunshine circled the table keeping to the eye corners of her new den, then lay down in a lump, not knowing or wondering where the hell Cloudy was.

He spent days removing mud and fencing from the congealing garden and hours tugging at the feral murk that seemed to pile within the Moorquoy's structure. From one hour to the next the house moved from a place of disaster, its earthen spew teetering at the door gap waiting to be flung in the trailer, to a space that looked like it was turning inside out, reaching back to some other where, almost a home again. He thought about the grade and incline of other people's years but not his and Kelly's. He wondered at the slow finishing that had been sucked from the owners of Moorquoy.

Over the following weeks he laboured while Sunshine fell through days. Eventually she got to sniff a new sofa and plunged into the emptied cardboard containers of corner book cases and new shelving – coming up she had polystyrene bits on her sticky nose end and for a minute or two happily biffed her muzzle sideways on the thick new rug until – as if remembering that to do this was at severe odds with her usual state of mope – she slunk off to lie down in the draughts.

And that night the Chapel's new dark green paint resisted its first blow, it romped in making the lights and radio fail together, along with, strangely enough, the tap water, which hissed to a last blank drip. Grant stood, gripping at the drenched towels he'd wedged on the windowsill as the bedevilled night zigged its nails over glass and tin. Sunshine snored through it though, and with her top lip back slightly, her sulphur coloured incisors poked out in unconscious defiance – at every new escalation of the storm's venom she let out an equally savage snort accompanied by rolling eyes and the odd scrabble of a paw on her basket's side.

Later, in an intense drained hour, a roof sheet yawed open and the gale tried to truly possess the chapel, Grant carried a now flustered Sunshine out to the car – thankful even, to be weighed down by any amount, on the twenty foot trip through the pelting and stabbing. Then he went back and had a mad half-hour trying to nail on a plank from the inside. After partly succeeding he too bailed out into the car which was sheltered by some ancient yelling alders.

They sat awake in the rocking vehicle with the radio coming through, a small vestige of sanity. Sunshine fidgeted between rations of biscuits and waited for the engine to be fired and for some trip to be undertaken

– though she would then have to be in the back with Cloudy, and he was hidden everywhere, so perhaps he was the warm heat coming from the floor, or the soft crunch of the biscuit in her mouth, he'd been in the other arm as she'd hung – a stuffed fluffed wad from this big dog's arm. Everywhere the creep of her mind fell – Cloudy turned and eyed and smelled and brushed against her, the great loudness in her heart which had only resonated in isolation now joined the earthly black shock of outside. Every time she looked at him he would be about to know, he would turn them to the lightness after all the long weighing and then with her neck released and the weight on her paws she might burst through a wall and bash into him again and again.

When two months had passed Grant thought hard about Kelly for a morning. Sitting outside on a pile of pristine wooden planks, the released land drying after weeks of nauseous rain, he watched Hoy island, the immense presence lying in the south. Every detail of its hulk connected to his eye – each of its ripped fissures tripping into alignment. He realized he had done everything to the chapel either as something Kelly would or would not do – her splinters were infecting the idea of the place, with them he would have to live, but Sunshine? – this surely wasn't the way. When he'd left it should have been without a wife spitting the dog upon him as a bitter farewell trophy.

That afternoon he took Sunshine back to Scotland on the Stromness ferry, then he drove five hundred miles to make a cold dog call in England – shouting inside after opening the door with an old key, pushing the sleepy dog through the gap and turning to scurry off as joyous barking came from behind the slammed door.

Kelly may have been in, out or dead, he didn't know. But he'd managed to unsnap something – something that belonged in another fold of entanglement.

Annie Harcus

Millie's manoeuvres

Energy fast and furious,
into the leaves she went.
One little terrier full of enthusiasm
enjoying freedom was the immediate intent.

As gentle breezes descended
swirling amongst undergrowth.
Excitement was evidently seen,
when four paws pounced with delight.

Snuffling, barking. What did she see?
An imaginary bone, or reality?
She appeared to be in earnest,
her tail wagging fast.
Was it worth the effort? Had she
found it at last?

Shaking and quaking with anticipation
in reverse gear she hauled it out.
A plastic bone, with bells inside. She proudly
presented the item, to echoes of doggy shouts.

Have we searched for something elusive?
Diligently sought with zeal?
'Tis very important to find Him.
God through Jesus revealed.

Our eternal future is very exciting.
Happiness for evermore.
Present ourselves before the only One
who can cleanse and make us whole.

Shout and sing from the rooftop.
Be diligent in searching God's word.
The father on high is observing
every action his subjects perform.

Jennifer MacRae

White halves

Smooth as a fingertip this pebble in my palm
grey line splits the two
I see
beyond the furthest point.

Break snap thunder black
pave grey crumbles down to darkening hue
the earth ledge trembles and shatters
trips my airless fall to blue
caught free by a triad of white horses
all winged
to ride from Hell to Heaven
while merry devil dances
on gossamer wings, I fly
above Heaven's high light
then merge to grey and vanish to white

Laura Watts

Gorgon's Kiss

From sun to red-end star
time's mason,
gravity,
fuses
hydrogen into helium;
our carbon flesh into nitrogen earth,
and silicon sand.

Beneath the Sun reborn,
the planet remade,
we are ground into a monument for the stars,
polished
by a race
whose kiss we will only know
as stone.

Jim Hewitson

Lambs by the Zillion

This has to be the scariest time of year for a boy brought up among the sandstone canyons of Clydebank.

The nearest we ever got to nature was helping oor neighbour sweep up the horse apples for his allotment after the scrappie's cairt passed by or oglin' the buxom Mistress K, three closes along, hinging, gloriously and enormously, from the windae, watchin' the world go by.

Scary, because here on the Atlantic edge lambs have started popping out all over the place. Being so far north and having had a seemingly endless winter, they wisely waited until the first half-hearted burst of sunshine illuminated Papa Westray. Nature is now running riot and the wee, woolly ones are arriving in droves.

Signs of imminent lambing on our isle are familiar enough. Crofters rush about the place peering over dykes; in the dead of night a strange, brightly-lit UFO (unidentified farming object) creeps below the Smithy Park (Neil on his night inspection)' the 'backies', the huge black-back gulls, hover over the field at Tirlo waiting to pick off the weaklings and wanderers (if it doesn't sound too blasphemous what WAS God thinking about when he created these dark predators?); and the 24-hour rota for lamb watch is organised and snatched sleep is now standard.

As we monitor the northern skies – for the drenching, withering showers can chill the life out of a new-born lamb – it's a sobering yet inspiring thought that this planning and anxiety must have been a part of everyday life for our predecessors who watched their flocks on this distant island, long before the Pyramids were built or Scotland as a nation was even thought of.

From midden remains at stone-built settlements like Skara Brae on mainland Orkney and our own Papay farmstead at the Knap of Howar (the oldest standing house in Europe) we know that sheep were raised with cattle and pigs.

Viking arrivals over 1000 years ago found numerous flocks dispersed around the Orkney archipelago, and are likely to have brought some of their own sheep with them when they settled. Wool combs have been discovered in Viking graves. By the 1500s Orkney sheep had gained a reputation as fearful breeders – three lambs being commonplace, foursomes occasionally. I wonder if there is bit of exaggeration here, twins being the norm these days?

Monitoring the expectant ewes would have been as important 6,000 years ago as it is today. Too long between the rounds might result in a 'hanging' case – a lamb dead with only the head showing. If a good milking ewe lost her lamb the skin would be flayed and put on an orphan lamb, which was then introduced to its new mother.

I also like to think that even without the benefit of glass bottles, drenches, powdered milk, and plastic teats, some 'caddie' or orphan lambs, would have been reared by the fireside in those Stone Age settlements as they are at School Place today.

Here on Papa Westray we have an added bonus. Across on the uninhabited Holm of Papay we can step back through millennia. Holland Farm has a flock of seaweed eating sheep, the scraggy, self-reliant 'bussy-broos' who look as if they might be blown away by the first zephyr. In fact, they are the hardiest of creatures and, according to the experts, probably very similar to the sheep of the Stone Age farmers.

The most unkind of Papay's farmers suggest that some of the Hewitson flock are so aged they must have experienced the Neolithic at first hand. We have no time for insults. A 'caddie' lamb in a cardboard box in front of the kitchen stove wants his tea.

Joanna Ramsey

Not over

I know
it must end.

Sell the house,
pack the books,

burn all
incriminating letters,

lock the door
for the last time,

stack the odds
between us –

eight hundred miles
of road,

fields of ripening
green,

a channel
of grey water –

opening my eyes
to a different sky,

only to find
I have not left behind

the lasting infidelity
of dreams.

Shadow
(for Chris)

Your sickness
has slipped
under my skin,

your sadness seeps
into the corners
of my eyes,

running out at the
edges of the night
and day,

all my images
of you overlain
by this new thing:

your unframed face
sharpened by pain
to a fine point.

(Acknowledgement to *Cutting Teeth*, where these poems first appeared.)

Netta of the islands

There had been a wedding at the kirk, and scraps of confetti lay between the flagstones as Netta walked to the ferry. She glanced up at the white doors, tightly shut. It was years since she had been inside, made wary by her father and then certain for herself that if there was a God, he had withdrawn his favour from her. Her father hated the church, although the Bible interested him greatly, and he frequently quoted from it, especially a verse from Psalm 105: 'And they took possession where others had toiled.' It confirmed his hatred of incomers, and he cited it as an example of divine unfairness, in a variety of arguments.

Once an Episcopalian minister came to the house, to consult him about some matter of local history. Netta, eavesdropping, soon heard the conversation turn to religion. Before long, out thundered the familiar words from the psalm.

'Where's the justice in that?' her father asked. 'You tell me that.'

Predictably, the minister's reply failed to satisfy him.

'A nimsy whimsy man,' he said scornfully, at supper.

The minister never came to the house again. He had left years ago. He hated the sea: hated the crossings between the scattered islands.

Now the boat forced its way through slate-coloured water. A boy hung his head over the side, sick as a dog. In the smoky cabin, German tourists flirted with local girls, inviting them to a party. Their voices were loud, but Netta ignored them. She stared ahead, mastering an expression of contempt. Tourists, her father said, were a necessary evil.

The hills were closer now and a wash of pale gold light showed between dull clouds. The boat cut its engines and swung in. Netta pushed ahead of the tourists and leapt out, ignoring the boatman's proffered hand. At the pier-head, a notice reminded visitors that some of this island's birds were protected species.

'Aye, and who'll protect the lambs?' Netta's aunt would rage at the bird warden, when she spotted him in the pub. She was a tiny, angry woman, who kept four hundred sheep on poor pasture.

'I've seen them buggers come in bloody flocks to pick the eyes oot of a sick beast. And noo you tell me I cannae shoot them!'

Some of the buggers were massing above the hills, as Netta strode along, hands in pockets. She came here to clear her head; to brood; to plot. She was a strong young woman, with coarse blonde hair and a sullen mouth. She had no husband, no child and no job. She lived with her parents in the house where she was born. Her father was well known for speaking his mind, not caring who he offended, and Netta took after him. Her mother was a little afraid of him, and perhaps of Netta too.

I wouldn't be like that, thought Netta, if I had a child. But to find a father for the child; that was the trick. She thought of the fishermen at the harbour, eyeing her as she boarded the ferry. Out of the question, as far as a husband was concerned. But how could she bring up a child without money of her own?

Oh, damn that man, she thought, remembering Donald, whom she had loved; damn him, who had seduced her – no, that was unfair: she had been willing – when she was sixteen. He had said they would be together. But at university he had fallen in love with an English girl, and married her, and never came back except to bring his wife and children to visit his parents each summer. Even now, the pain of missing Donald – his voice and the feel of his body – had the power to wrench at Netta's guts.

She looked around, at the bog cotton, and buttercups fringing the ditch, and sheep grazing. The lower road threaded through an outbreak of new bungalows with pebbledash walls. This road was deserted, winding past a tumbledown cottage and petering into a track; she felt stones through her soles. She saw the glint of water in the loch. A great skua swished down; she waved her fist at it. Bloody vicious birds.

In better times, her father owned a house here. Every Easter and summer they came, and it was heaven. To go without shoes, to run in the meadows and on the beach in complete freedom. There is no heaven, her father told her; this is all you get. But it was enough.

He had been proud of her then. The future had seemed simple: school; college; teaching music. Music was in her blood, her fingertips: it was her need and her gift. She would go away to study and come home to pass on her knowledge, in the only place she cared for. But it had not turned out well. When Donald broke with her, she lost heart, scraping through her studies instead of shining, and lost her grip on the world. She could not keep up. Her smile slipped, and she became sullen and set. She didn't get the job she wanted. There were bits and pieces of work

– supply teaching; a few private pupils. Sometimes she forced herself to do other jobs: serving in a shop – but customers didn't like her – or cleaning, but that never lasted, because her employers said she thought herself above the work.

Last year, Annie Anderson retired. Everyone knew the assistant music teacher would get her job, no matter how much they advertised. But that left the assistant's post vacant, and Netta saw her way in at last. But she hadn't got it! That bloody English woman had sailed in and taken it. Netta felt poisoned by hatred of her, and all her kind, who took possession where others had worked and hoped. Netta had seen the woman yesterday, working in her garden. She had her own house, and a lilac tree and a hedge of flowering currant.

Once, at a concert in the town hall, the new teacher came in at the last minute and sat, annoyingly, in front of Netta, blocking her view. Who did she think she was, in her long coat and her silver earrings? There was no escaping her: she even tried to speak to Netta in the interval, as they sat shifting their backsides on the plastic chairs, asking if she could look at Netta's programme. Netta held it out in silence, her mouth at its most sullen, before getting to her feet and going to sit at the back.

They came here, people like that, transplanting themselves with apparent ease. They didn't adapt: they just went on living their messy, snobby lives, but in a bonnier place. They brought their stupid ideas with them, about animals and birds and 'the environment', when they didn't have the faintest idea about the realities of rural life. They trampled on the old ways; they smoothed over the beautiful old cracks.

When Netta was a child, she knew every face she passed in the street, and walked to school without fear of traffic or strange men. Now children trailed behind their anxious mothers, flattening themselves against the wall as cars rattled past. You never knew who anybody was these days. Nothing was safe. And the voices, along the street and in the shops: how often did you hear good broad dialect, local words and intonations? She remembered the old days and wanted to weep. The dear old shops, their windows enlarged now and signs lit and names changed, like any bloody high street in any mainland town.

Her breath came in short bursts, as much from agitation as from the gradient of the track, which narrowed at the shoulder of the hill.

After a few more strides she saw the enclosed valley, the stream amongst rowan trees. Birds flew up from the heather, almost under her feet. Another skua grazed her scalp and she swore at it, lashing out. Even this valley was changed, for in summer the path was often busy with walkers. Tourists had discovered her private place. A film director had built a house here, and brought guests: foreigners, weird arty people who drove too fast in large cars.

Below her, the mouth of the valley opened out to the bay. Netta's heart quickened: this was the place she would kill for; die for; her inheritance. Her father's family came from this valley, generations of them. Her chest felt sore; it was too long since she had made this climb. They said these cliffs were almost the highest in Europe.

As she neared her usual vantage point, her heart sank. Someone was there before her, in her place. On the sheltered ledge where the crumbling earth had slipped a few feet, a woman sat facing the sea, her hair whipping in the wind. It was the music teacher. Netta felt herself grow cold with anger. She moved closer, thinking: she hasn't heard me, she doesn't know I'm here. I could push her so easily, one hand in the middle of her back.

But intuition made the woman turn, revealing a white, wet face: she had been crying.

'I just stopped to look at the view,' she said uncertainly, wiping her tears with the back of her hand. 'You can see the mainland from here.' As if, for God's sake, Netta didn't know. 'I come here when I'm homesick: it looks so close on a fine day. Not today, though.'

The mainland hills were lost under low cloud. Netta grudgingly sat above the ledge where the woman perched like a bird. A fulmar sheered past, its wings tilting.

'What made you come, if you miss your home so much?' Netta meant the question to sound scornful, but it came out gently.

'Just chance,' the woman said. 'It was the first job that came up, after I made the decision to leave. It could have been anywhere.' Her voice was sad.

'And why did you decide to leave?'

The woman shrugged, inside her big jacket.

'Oh, how many reasons do you need? Too many years of city life. A messed-up marriage. Being mugged.'

Impulsively she unzipped her collar and pulled it open, to reveal a puckering of the skin on her neck: an angry reddish mark that suggested violent impact.

'I just wanted to get as far away as possible.'

If I'm supposed to feel pity, thought Netta, I don't.

'I don't see why you had to choose here!' she burst out.

'Why not, Netta?'

'You know my name!'

'Of course I do.'

'Well, then – because it's my place. My place and my job.'

'I wondered when we would come to that,' the woman said, as if to herself.

'My job,' Netta went on, 'that I was waiting for. If you hadn't come they'd have given it to me.'

The woman stared at Netta's angry mouth.

'Not necessarily,' she said. 'Not from what I've heard. Don't make me the scapegoat for your failures.'

'What do you know about my failures?' shouted Netta, longing to beat her fists against that pale city face.

'I don't know much. Some gossip, that's all.'

Netta was disconcerted. She blustered, to regain control.

'You just take, take, take, like all your kind. You don't even try to fit in.'

'It's not easy fitting in,' the woman said, 'when people aren't friendly.'

Netta did not reply.

'I've been here six months,' the woman said. 'Hardly anyone has bothered to find out anything about me. Only a few people have offered me a meal, a fireside, a conversation.'

'And who would they be?'

'One or two of the other teachers. And Harold. He's been kind.'

Harold Mathers was the nearest thing the islands had to a local celebrity. He was an artist, a painter who had exhibited successfully in Edinburgh and beyond. His old croft was stuffed with books and pictures, and he lived there alone, never having married. There were various stories about him and local women.

'Well, I suppose you're young, and quite bonny,' Netta said contemptuously. 'And he's too old to know any better.'

'You won't spoil the friendship by sneering. It's all the same to him, where I come from. I can talk to him, and he tells me things. He says, come down, the kettle's on, and I've that terrible cake my daughter sent.'

'He has a daughter?' Netta exclaimed.

'Yes. In Lancashire. Why didn't you know that, Netta? She sends him food parcels, great lumps of fruitcake in brown paper. The point is,' she went on, 'that people are free to come and go. You could have gone.'

The sea heaved below, grey marbled with white. Netta pulled at a tuft of sea-pinks which clung to the loose soil.

'My family has been here for ever!' she said defiantly.

'Your father's family, yes, And your mother was born here, I know. But your grandmother came from Wales. Harold told me. That's a fine inheritance. Why be ashamed of it?'

'I'm not ashamed! Of course not.'

'But it spoils your argument, doesn't it? You see, I do know something about you. I asked Harold. I bothered to find out. I could see you hated me.'

'I don't hate you,' Netta said dully, realising it was true. Could she not succeed even in her resolution to despise this woman? 'I hate the idea of you.'

She struggled to sound reasonable.

'Incomers are welcome here. It's when they impose their ways, and take our jobs and houses. I hate change. I hate it.'

It had begun to drizzle. The music teacher shivered.

'I'm cold. I need to get moving.'

She reached for her rucksack.

'Don't worry,' she said. 'I shan't stay. I could never be happy here. Perhaps you'll get your job. Harold would speak up for you, you know. He likes you.'

She scrambled to her feet, hoisting the rucksack onto her back. She's too near the edge, thought Netta. She watched the woman lose her balance and step backwards into the air. Her face wore an expression of complete amazement as the wind took her.

One fine evening, Netta saw Harold leaning on his stick, at the woman's grave. Not that there was much left to bury, when they found her. Netta waved and Harold raised his stick in greeting, so she went to stand beside him.

'She was a fine woman,' Harold said. 'You might have liked her, if you'd taken the trouble to speak to her.'

'Maybe I would,' Netta answered, 'but we'll never know.'

'Come down one night?' Harold suggested, poking his stick at a weed which had sprung up by the headstone. 'Come and have a dram. Tell me what's going on up at the school.'

'I might,' said Netta.

She smiled at him, her face hopeful in the dazzle of low light, which cast long shadows over the flattened turf.

An earlier version of this story was published in *The New Shetlander*.

Pamela Beasant

Missing from the picture

The bowl's interior,
creamy white, with a
spiralling red stripe
to follow with your
finger, endlessly,
always contained
tomato soup.
Gran's favourite.

But in the photograph
of the place we sat to eat it,
there's an empty table
drawn back chair.

When I'm gone,
who will place the outline
of child, gran, soup bowl
in the picture?
How many lost outlines
in every picture
must there be?

Gran's arthritic hand
wiped the table clean;
now it's as if the slow,
repeated moment's
never been.

Parted by the Atlantic

You sit by the ocean
I sit by the sea.
Walk in. You'll find
there's no need to breathe.
Walk on the sea-bed
at the base of the undersea
mountains. Walk
round them.
I'll sit here
until your head emerges
seal-like, watching
from your ocean, my sea.

(This poem appears in
Running with a snow leopard,
Two Ravens Press, 2008.)

i.m. Gunnie Moberg, 1941-2007

G old on the Black Craig as the sun dips
U nder the horizon's rim to a
N ew day somewhere else. I wished you
N ot that last fierce dark ravagement, but
I ncrements of strength. Now your
E ffervescent spirit burns absent, like the sun's disc.

John McGill

Noble rot

'*Elefantenrennen,*' the elderly man said.

The young man frowned.

The elderly man turned his head to look at him, then back to watch the road. 'Elephant racing. When two or three of these monsters are together on the motorway.'

The young man understood. 'Ah, the lorries.'

The elderly man glanced at the speedometer. A comfortable hundred. He laughed. '*Elefantenrennen.* I suppose there's still some creativity to be found - I think we tend to be too pessimistic about young people and their language.'

The young man knew a reply was expected. 'Maybe,' he said.

'Of course it might be different in English, with the American influence,' the elderly man said.

'Possibly.'

' "Might" be different: "may" be different - should it have been "may"? I'm never sure of the distinction.'

'I don't think it matters much,' the young man said. 'I think it's a sort of grey area.'

The elderly man sighed. 'Ah, yes, it all seems to be grey nowadays, and so.... unwitty. *Audi* is an interesting little story - you know it?'

'No,' the young man said.

'There's was a large engineering firm called *Horch*. You get it?'

'*Horch*?'

'Yes, but they had too many bad relationships, they became too much associated with the regime, so the name was changed. And you see how they did it?'

The young man thought. 'Ah yes,' he said.

'You see? They simply translated it into Latin.'

'Hark,' the young man said.

'Pardon?'

'Hark.'

'I don't know it.'

'It's old-fashioned. Poetic. It means "listen".'

'Listen, yes. Quite clever, I think.'

The young man agreed that it was clever.

'I don't suppose there's much Latin in English schools nowadays,' the elderly man said.

'Not much.'

'No. It's the same here, small Latin and less Greek. I'm horrified to think of the future - only the other day I discovered that just four of my class ten could recite the Greek alphabet, and one of them could only do it because he's an astronomer, and apparently it's of some use there. And that's in a *Gymnasium*. My hopes are very low.'

'Times change,' the young man said.

'Too much, and too fast, perhaps,' the elderly man said. 'You notice most of the traffic is coming from the opposite direction?'

'Yes.'

'That's the Convention. They're expecting a very big attendance, perhaps one million for the final rally. But 1 suppose you are a socialist of some kind?'

The young man shrugged apologetically. 'Where I come from,' he said.

'Yes. I shall be there tomorrow. I think I have to make a speech, or something.'

'A million people,' the young man said,

'Yes, if the weather is nice. Not all young people are bitten by the Marxist bug nowadays, in fact it's getting almost unfashionable.'

The young man changed the subject. 'It looks promising enough today.'

'Yes, I think we'll be lucky this time. And it's lucky that tomorrow is the Long Saturday, we can be more carefree. Last year it was a Thursday, I seem to remember.'

'I think so.'

'This time we can be more relaxed, we don't have to home quite so early. I think you bought one or two cases last year?'

'Yes. A couple of *Kabinetts* and one *Spätlese*.'

The elderly man sighed again. 'I find it one of the few civilised things left.'

'We shall soon be passing the exit for Limburg. You remember it from last year?'

The young man remembered it well. 'A nice town,' he said.

'You think so? I always find it just a bit overdone, just slightly Mickey-Mouse.'

The young man smiled. 'Where I come from.'

'Well, yes. Glasgow, isn't it? Or Edinburgh?'

'Glasgow.'

'Yes, Glasgow. I've never been. On my last visit to Scotland I went only as far as Abbotsford. For me it was a pilgrimage, I suppose.'

When the young man said nothing, he continued with a hint of rebuke in his voice, 'You don't like Scott?'

'I hardly know him,' the young man confessed. `I think I finished *Redgauntlet* but I gave up on Rob Roy when he still hadn't turned up at page two hundred.'

The elderly man tutted. 'For me he's something of an obsession. I've been working on a translation of *Anne of Geierstein* for about twenty years, on and off - purely as a hobby, of course, I don't intend it for publication. You might like to look at one or two pages.'

The young man said he would, though he didn't know the book He felt the wickedness coming on again, like last year. Remembering a punishment inflicted upon him by a whimsical teacher, he said, 'I think critical opinion is moving away from Scott now - to people like William Creech.'

'Who?'

'William Creech. A bit older than Scott, same generation as Burns.'

The elderly man was interested. 'William Creech? How is that written?' The young man spelled it.

'Mm - I don't know him. I must look for him - did he write novels?'

'Mostly poems. His stature's been growing steadily.'

'Really?'

Wickedly, the young man recited the lines he had written five hundred times:

'*Traverse the world and fly from pole to pole!*
Go far as winds can blow or waters roll!
Lo! All is vanity beneath this sun,
To silent death through heedless paths we run.'

'Yes,' the elderly man said. 'I must look him up. I have a lot of anthologies.'

The whimsical teacher had resorted to minor rhymesters as providing sterner punishment than the tawse. Ashamed of the wickedness the young man said, 'There's the Limburg exit.'

'Ah yes. It was one of my exploits as a student, to row down the Lahn from Marburg, through Limburg, to the Rhine.'

'Really? An adventure.'

'Yes. I was a keen oarsman, I rowed a lot as a schoolboy, with the Youth Organisation. It's an attractive little river. We leave the motorway now, and take the *Bundesstrasse,* and then I think it's nicer to go by the side-roads, do you agree?'

The young man agreed.

'Very soon you will see a most unusual traffic sign,' the elderly man said. 'Perhaps you remember it from last year?'

'Oh yes,' the young man said. 'The snakes. The non-poisonous crossers.'

'Precisely. I've many times thought about stopping at this place and watching for a while. I've never actually seen one here, but I have heard stories involving hundreds of them,'

'Schlangenbad,' the young man read from the sign. 'Snake Spa.'

The elderly man smiled. 'Yes, one of these times we must pause and watch them taking the waters. Should it be "watch them *take,*" *or* "watch them *taking*"?'

'Grey again,' the young man said.

The elderly man patted the armrest of the wooden bench. 'You see the initials?' he said.

The young man leaned across. 'J...W...G,' he read. 'Goethe?'

The elderly man nodded. 'Spurious, of course - just a late nineteenth century joke of some sort, but quite interesting in its own right, don't you think?'

'The bench seems old enough,' the young man said.

'Oh yes - comfortably. Mid-eighteenth century at the latest, exactly the right period. And he did visit the region. He stayed in a house just by the river, the home of a certain Herr Bretano.'

'I believe he was quite fond of the wine,' the young man ventured.

'Oh yes, yes, two or three bottles a day - but the red Franconian wines were his favourite tipple. Is that correct - "tipple"? - is that the word?'

The young man said it was.

The elderly man pointed towards the river. 'He stayed in another place not far from here - the inn at Lahnstein, just round the bend of the river, where he was much impressed by the castle.'

The young man was drowsy, but the elderly man wanted to practise his English.

'I find it irritating that he should receive so much attention, while others are ignored or even dismissed - it upsets me.'

The young man shrugged. 'Icons,' he said.

'Perhaps, yes,' the elderly man said. 'But 1 can't help feeling it should have been Klopstock. Or Hagedorn - why has no one heard of Hagedorn, nowadays? Or Gellert? Perhaps even you have not heard of them?'

'Only vaguely,' the young man said. 'Only as names.'

'I'm not surprised. There's been a tendency to belittle them as insignificant anacreontic scribblers, and to assume that nothing happened before Klopstock, don't you think?'

'Well...'

'As if wit and cleverness had somehow become sinful,' the elderly man interrupted. 'You know what I mean?'

'Well, it's not so very different...'

'Gellert is always witty.' The elderly man put his hand to his brow, recollecting.

' *Wenn deine Schrift dem Kenner nicht gefällt*
So ist es schon ein böses Zeichen:
Doch wenn sie gar des Narren Lob erhält:
So ist es Zeit, sie auszustreichen.'

The young man shut his eyes, translating, and the elderly man helped him. 'It's a bad thing when the expert doesn't like your work, but when the fool praises it, then it's time to stroke it out.'

He reached out his right hand, fingers spread. 'The view from here explains everything, you see? In this part you can see that it is flowing not south to north, but east to west, so that this bank faces south.'

'Yes.'

'And the other factor is correct too - the slope is perfect, so that one has the direct heat of the sun and the reflected heat from the river.'

'It's very warm today,' the young man said.

'Indeed. That's the third factor - the climate here is exceptionally mild, and the hills offer protection from the northern wind. The whole region used to be cut off, so they say - surounded by a great hedge.'

'*Dornröschen.*'

'Precisely. Briar Rose. There is much truth in these old things, though there is a fashion now for dismissing the Grimm Brothers. You have another word, don't you? Not "dismissing"?'

'Debunking.'

'Debunking, yes, that's it, everyone is debunking nowadays. I find it becomes monotonous. The autumn here is normally mild and undramatic.'

'Mists and mellow fruitfulness,' the young man said.

'Indeed, fruitfulness is exactly correct - this is an area of exceptionally fine fruit. Of course a lot of nonsense is talked. It's no doubt true that the soil here is heavy and rich compared with the Mosel, but the differences are exaggerated.'

'The Mosel is slatey,' the young man said.

'Quite. And there are so many twists and turns, so many micro-climates. There are some who swear by Mosel; for my part, I think it's all purely personal.'

'I like all of them,' the young man said

'Quite, quite. De gustibus non est disputandum. Which is not to deny that there are special years. I have still at home one or two of the *79 Auslese* from here - generally considered to be the best vintage since the War.'

'Oh?'

'Yes. I used to come here two or three times in the year, when the old count was alive. I knew him from away back, when we used to make camping trips in the Taunus, with the Youth Organisation. Now his son is the owner, and I have very little in common with him. The tastings used to be wonderful occasions.'

The young man started a yawn, stifled it.

'I think you're beginning to suffer a little from the heat,' the elderly man said.

'A bit.'

'It's fortunate that we had such a light snack. And I seem to think you've been rather more careful with your tasting this time, no? Not too much swallowing.'

The young man laughed. 'And plenty of water.' he said.

They stood up, and the young man blinked.

The elderly man sniffed. 'This place is government-owned now, but I think you can still feel the presence of the monks.'

'I remember that smell,' the young man said.

'Yes, the *Edelfäule* - a rather beautiful oxymoron, don' t you think?' the elderly man said. 'How would it be in English?'

'*Noble rot*, I suppose - but I'm not sure there's anything specially oxymoronic.'

'Ah-ha. I forgot you are a socialist" The elderly man licked his lips. *Noble rot*. Yes, a pleasant name for a disease,'

'*Edelfäule* sounds even rottener,' the young man said.

'In the late autumn you can smell it more strongly,' the elderly man said. 'And there is always a pleasing coolness in the cloisters.'

'I remember,' the young man said.

'Yes. An olfactory experience, I believe you called it.'

The young man had been practising his German the previous year. He nodded and said, '*Eine Geruchserfahrung.*'

'I've placed it here. On this wall,' the elderly man said.

'Ah.' The young man stepped towards the wall.

'This is magnified, of course - four times the actual size. You can see that this side is rather worn, which made it a little less expensive than these things usually are.'

'That side's perfect,' the young man said.

'Yes. The definition is very good. You can see the owl in great detail, and the letters.'

The young man read, 'Alpha, theta, epsilon.' He liked astronomy,

'Yes, that's the normal inscription on Athenian pieces. This is a tetradrachma. I'm having a few of them re-photographed. Is that a legitimate word - "re-photographed"?'

The young man nodded. 'Fine,' he said. 'And the originals - you keep them in the bank?'

'In a safe-deposit.'

'Don't you ever get an urge to look at them - handle them a bit?'

'Ah yes, I sometimes have a small yearning, but it's best not to handle them too often, of course.'

They sat down on the sofa and the young man sipped the last dreg of the seventy-nine *Auslese*. The elderly man refilled his glass.

'It's very good.' the young man said.

'I thought you might like it - I think it is at its optimum age now, perhaps just beginning to decline.'

'I know the feeling,' the young man said.

'Pardon?' The elderly man frowned.

'Oh, just a bad joke,' the young man said.

The elderly man smiled. 'Ah. Yes, a joke. Humour is a strange thing.'

'It doesn't translate well,' the young man said.

The elderly man agreed. 'No, I suppose not. I remember we all used to laugh at Chaplin, but then we hadn't much else, there wasn't much to compare him with.'

'I think a lot of people still laugh at him,' the young man said.

'Yes, Chaplin. But other things - the Marx Brothers, for example; frankly, I could never see what people found to be amused at.'

'De gustibus...' the young man said.

The elderly man nodded. 'I suppose I find myself out of key with what passes as funny nowadays, in fact I find myself depressed by the decline in standards almost everywhere, though I don't expect you'll agree.'

'Times change,' the young man said, and drained his glass.

'Now we can try just a little of this,' the elderly man said. 'I think you will find it quite acceptable.'

The young man tried to read the label.

'This is the *Trockenbeerenauslese* from seventy-five,' the elderly man said as he poured.

The young man held his glass against the light from the wall-lamp. 'It looks like olive oil,' he said.

The elderly man held his own glass under his nose, sniffed gently, nodded. 'Only last Sunday I saw something that struck me as very typical, at the crossing, beside the *Volksbank,* you know the place?'

The young man knew it well. 'Yes, it's my bank.'

'A couple, hardly in their thirties, with two children, arrived at the crossing and marched them across without the slightest regard for the signal. I was standing on the opposite side with an old lady. She gave them a piece of her mind when they arrived at our side, but they only laughed in her face.'

'Was there any traffic?' the young man asked.

'No, as it chanced, the road was clear, that was the point, I suppose: they saw it was clear and that was enough. No thought for the children, no thought for the terrible example they were showing.'

'No.'

'I didn't speak to the old lady, but we exchanged a look of despair. These were not silly youths or *Gastarbeiter* - they were a professional couple. I thought I might use the story tomorrow, at the Convention, somehow it seems to summarise things.'

The young man shook his glass, the lamplight danced.

The elderly man continued. 'It's the lack of respect for authority, the feeling that you only need to obey the rules when it suits your own immediate purpose, that you have no obligation to your children. You know what 1 mean?'

'Yes.'

'Or am I just being an old fogey?'

'Not at all.'

'We learned it from so many different sources - parents, school, the church, the Youth Organisation; even our older brothers and sisters.'

'Tempora mutantur,' the young man said, dipping his tongue into his wine. 'Times change.' The sweetness passed unimpeded from his upper lip to his knees. He leaned back on the sofa; if he tried to stand up he would fall. Behind the elderly man's back he had drunk eighteen glasses of wine during their trip, then six more as his guest. He swallowed a minute drop of the seventy-nine *Trockenbeerenauslese* and felt it stop somewhere in his chest. Olive oil. In the street or at home he would have joyously surrendered to the urge to vomit. Here, sharing a sofa with an elderly man who wore a striped suit and patent-leather shoes in his own sitting-room, by his own fireside, that option was closed.

He gulped hard, forcing the oiliness through the knot in his diaphragm.

'One thing I wanted to ask,' he said. 'One thing I've been thinking about.'

'Oh?' the elderly man said.

'Yes, just the one thing, the one wee thing....'

The elderly man waited.

Speaking into his wine, so that his voice reverberated in the glass, releasing the words slowly to avoid slurring, the young man said.

'I wanted… to know about this… Youth Organisation… I wanted to know about it… what it was called?'

Nellie and Rolf

Nellie, you pulled the chain
expecting no flush, you touched wood twice
before you spoke, sniffed rain
in sapphire skies, fainted at mice.
Every squeak you heard was rat.
And secretly you hoped the world was flat.

Remember the bus-stop, how barely on
you worried about getting off,
were lonely with your ulcer gone,
heard cancer in the thinnest cough?
And when I told you Mars was red,
'Tsch, tsch, that's terrible,' you said.

'At least I won't get fat,'
you said, 'You won't see fat on me,
I worry too much for that.'
And sure enough at sixty-three
you kept the space between your thighs,
the worried ankles and the rabbit eyes.

All monster your world, all attack,
all glass about to break,
all men in plimsolls at your back,
all big bad wolf and snake.
Action was sinful, life was sad,
no news was good and moving bad.

Then Rolf, who did what hippos do,
notwithstanding brick and tile,
and in a tidy German zoo
fashioned his Nile.
Rolf. Grossly there, most grossly male,
farter and snorter on the grand scale.

His house was barely hippo-size,
his bath all straining at the seams,
and yet he wallowed to the eyes
and in his hippo-dreams,
all fart and snort and grunt and groan,
took flight above the spires of Cologne.

Translating from the sign
I told you not to be upset
by muck: hippos, it said, feel fine
in water dyed by hippo-shit.
You blanched at the picture, shuffled your feet,
but let me steer you through the hippo-heat.

Nothing. A cavern of hot fat stink.
You leaned across the railing of his tub.
'He's somewhere out the back, I think,'
you said, and gave your eyes a rub.
Then thunderously beneath your nose,
Rolf the mighty spluttered forth and rose.

Oh Nellie how you laughed and nearly died,
and saw your maker in that hippo-head,
'Dear God in Heaven, that's terrible,' you cried.
And HHRRMMFF and SPLUTTERHHRRMMFF he said.
HHRRMMFF he said then HHRRMMFF and SPLUTTERFART,
piercing you Nellie to your rabbit-heart.

Yvonne Gray

Reflections
(for Sylvia Wishart)

In the window the sky is darkening.
Tall cliffs breach the restless sea.
A curlew jabs its beak in the earth
pegging down the billowing slope.
An owl hangs
stopped in the wind
then sweeps off over the stubble.

In the window a bowl of fruit is ripening.
Held in a bottle
a barque flies on bellying sails.
The reflection of a woman
lingers. Lovely still, she stands looking
at all she sees.

In the window the sky is darkening.
The field is harvested
the plough left to rust.
A hare dances
then leaps away.

(This poem appears in the collection *In the Hanging Valley*,
Two Ravens Press, March 2008.)

Lightness

As I climb the slope with the sledge in tow
clouds gather; the sky turns grey.
I see light prints of a hare in snow.

Far down on the shore below
a whale lies still at the edge of the bay.
I climb the slope with the sledge in tow.

At the brow of the hill I brace then let go –
runners scatter ice in a crystal spray.
I follow light prints of a hare in snow.

Out on the skyline, prow towards Faroe,
a container ship slips along the seaway.
I climb the slope with the sledge in tow.

On the coast beyond Hoy, lying low,
the puffball globe of Dounreay.
The prints of the hare are lost in snow.

My feet fall heavy and deep and slow –
the sky is like lead; the sea turns grey.
I climb the slope with the sledge in tow
seeking light prints of a hare in snow.

Editor's notes on contributors

John Aberdein is a poet and an award-winning novelist who often writes in his native Doric. He lives on Hoy, where he is working on a new novel.

Alex Ashman was born and brought up in Orkney. She is an art student at Duncan of Jordanstone in Dundee, specialising in animation.

Freda Bayne is a weaver and designer. She lives in Stromness and is currently working on a series of pieces made from North Ronaldsay wool, inspired by stories from the island.

Pam Beasant lives and works in Stromness. Her collection *Running with a Snow Leopard* was published by Two Ravens Press in January 2008.

Frances Bell lives on Sanday. She attended a writing workshop there, where she produced her contribution for this book.

Galen Brown is still at school and is already an award-winning inventor. He writes poetry and is working on a novel.

Diana Clay lives on Sanday. A former GP, she has been writing poetry for many years. She read her work most recently at the Shore to Shore festival.

Elizabeth Coward, originally from USA, lives in Stromness. She teaches at Stromness Academy and is a founding member of the Stromness writing group.

Christine De Luca, originally from Shetland, is now a core member of the Edinburgh Shore Poets. She has won many prizes for her poetry, which she writes in English and Shetlandic.

John Edmondson lives in Ireland and is a regular visitor to Orkney. He produced his contribution to this book at a workshop on Sanday.

Mike Fairbairn is a musician and song-writer. He's a regular member of the Stromness writing group.

Bill Ferguson lives in Sandwick and works as a court officer, a steward and a taxi driver. He is an integral part of the Stromness writing group and is working on a novel.

Ron Ferguson, former minister of St Magnus Cathedral, is a journalist, biographer and poet, with many books to his name. He writes columns for *The Herald, The Press and Journal* and *Orkney Today*.

Alison Flett is an award-winning poet and fiction writer who has read her work all over Scotland and beyond. She was recently awarded a Scottish Arts Council bursary, and has completed her first novel.

Becky Ford works at Stromness Library. She is the co-ordinator of the Stromness writing group, is studying for an OU degree, and writes both poetry and prose.

Clare Gee, originally from Hartlepool, is an artist and arts development officer/ manager of museums and heritage for OIC. She co-founded the Untitled group of artists.

Yvonne Gray is a poet, oboe player with Orkney Camerata and English teacher. Her collection *In the Hanging Valley* was published by Two Ravens Press in March 2008.

Emma Grieve was born and brought up in Orkney. She lives in Harray and is an English teacher at Stromness Academy.

Annie Harcus lives on Westray. She started writing when she retired and has published several pieces of poetry.

Sylvia Hays, originally from southern USA, has lived in Orkney for many years. She is an established artist, whose writing is achieving recognition.

Sally Heddle lives in Holm. A retired music teacher, she has a strong interest in creative writing, and is also a keen singer.

Ella Henderson grew up on North Ronaldsay. After a long teaching career in the south of England, she now lives in Stromness.

Jim Hewitson lives on Papa Westray. In a long writing career he has published poetry, fiction and journalism and is a regular contributor to BBC Radio Orkney.

Fran Flett Hollinrake lives in Stromness and runs Dragon History Tours. She's an essential member of the Stromness writing group and is working on a novel.

Diana Hendry has had a distinguished writing career and visited Orkney with the Edinburgh Shore Poets. Her latest collection is published by Peterloo Poets in 2008.

Laureen Johnson writes in Shetlandic and gave her first Orkney reading in 2007. She co-edits *The New Shetlander* with Brian Smith.

Lynn Johnson is a librarian at Orkney Library. She is working on an historical novel and is a stalwart of the Stromness writing group.

Dave Linklater lives in Kirkwall and plays the accordion with various groups all over Orkney.

LC Littlejohn is a regular columnist for *Orkney Today*, and has written many stories and articles. She is a core member of the Kirkwall writing group.

Ian McDonough is a leading member of Edinburgh Shore Poets. He read in Orkney in 2007 as part of the Shore to Shore festival.

John McGill's second novel was published in 2007 by Two Ravens Press. He has also published a collection of short stories, and has taught English and German.

Fiona MacInnes is an artist, poet, fiction writer and teacher. She lives in Stromness, runs a summer café on Hoy, and has just completed her first novel.

Morag MacInnes is a poet and an award-winning short story writer. Her collection, based on the extraordinary story of Isobel Gunn, is published by Hansel Cooperative Press in 2008.

Lesley McLeod lives in Kirkwall. She is a violinist with Orkney Camerata and Three in a Bar, and has many music pupils.

Jennifer MacRae is studying for a cultural studies degree at Orkney College. She co-mounted an exhibition of Orkney writers in 2007 at Tankerness House.

Gordon Marriott is a scientist who lives in Birsay. He has been experimenting with a novel and is a regular part of the Stromness writing group.

Paul Maxton is a solicitor with OIC. He recently returned to writing after a long break, and is putting together a collection of short stories.

Dorrie Morrison, originally from London, has lived in Stromness for many years. She has previously published a collection of poems.

Andrew Motion, the Poet Laureate, visited Orkney for the first time in 2007 as the St Magnus Festival's resident poet. He founded the acclaimed poetry archive project.

Alistair Peebles is a writer and photographer, who left a teaching career to branch out into publishing and gallery-curating. He opened the Porteous Brae Gallery in Stromness in 2007.

Andrew Philip is based in Linlithgow. He is a member of the Edinburgh Shore Poets and visited Orkney in 2007 to read at the Shore to Shore festival.

Joanna Ramsey's poetry and short stories have been widely published. She lives in Stromness, where she writes and edits in between other jobs.

Olive Ritch, born and brought up in Orkney, has been widely published as a poet and commended in the National Poetry Competition. She is studying creative writing at Aberdeen University.

Cathy Scott, a retired nurse, attended a workshop in North Ronaldsay where she produced her contribution to this book.

K.K. Scott, originally from USA, is a screenwriter and a core member of the Kirkwall writing group. She read her work at the Shore to Shore festival in 2007.

Sinclair Scott, former vice-convener of OIC and native of North Ronaldsay, attended a workshop on the island where he produced the piece in this book.

Doreen Sinclair is a regular member of the Kirkwall writing group. She most recently read at the Shore to Shore festival in 2007.

Margaret Storr used to write exam papers for students of English as a foreign language. She regularly attends the Kirkwall writing group.

Anne Thomson, originally from Glasgow, now lives in Stromness. She has been widely published as a poet and runs the Galdragon Press.

Roderick Thorne, photographer and former head-teacher at Sanday Junior High, is now an island Ranger. He produced his contribution to this book at a workshop on the island.

Kate Townsend grew up in England and now lives on Eday, where she is the island's development officer for OIC. She has had work published locally.

Helga Tulloch grew up in Stromness and has North Ronaldsay roots. She has recently completed her teacher training.

Laura Watts is a social anthropologist at Lancaster University, working on her PhD thesis. She visited Orkney for a few weeks in 2007.

Nigel Wheale, former university lecturer, has published academic books as well as poetry collections. He lives in Stromness and works at St Peter's House.

Hamish Whyte is a widely published poet. He runs the Mariscat Press in Edinburgh, and visited Orkney with the Shore Poets in 2007.

Bill Wilson, amongst many other activities, is president of the Stromness Debating Society, and a stalwart of the Kirkwall writing group. His prose has been previously published in *Living Orkney*.